I.S.A.M. Monographs: Number 14

The Phonograph and Our Musical Life

PROCEEDINGS OF A CENTENNIAL CONFERENCE
7-10 December 1977

Edited by H. Wiley Hitchcock

I.S.A.M. Monographs: Number 14

The Phonograph and Our Musical Life

PROCEEDINGS OF A CENTENNIAL CONFERENCE
7-10 December 1977

Edited by H. Wiley Hitchcock

Institute for Studies in American Music
Department of Music
School of Performing Arts
Brooklyn College
of The City University of New York

Library of Congress Catalog Card No. 80-82409
ISBN 0-914678-14-0

Printed in the United States of America

Published by Institute for Studies in American Music
Department of Music, School of Performing Arts,
Brooklyn College of the City University of New York
Brooklyn, New York 11210

CONTENTS

FOREWORD

This book is the written record of a conference, titled as is the book, held at Brooklyn College of the City University of New York, 7-10 December 1977, under the sponsorship of the Institute for Studies in American Music, with support from the National Endowment for the Humanities. The conference, timed to coincide with the centenary of the invention of the phonograph by Thomas Alva Edison on 7 December 1877, sought to explore the immense and pervasive influence that the phonograph, phonorecords, tape recordings, and related electronic developments have had on every segment of the musical community—audiences, composers, performers, scholars and critics, and other media (from radio, television, and films through libraries and museums to hotel elevators and airplane cabins). None of us has escaped being affected, in diverse and deep ways, by the phonograph and sound recording in general, and our musical experiences, perceptions, and horizons have been profoundly altered as a result. The aim of the conference was to search out, by explication and discussion among individuals of widely varying backgrounds and emphases in music, the nature of this impact.

The chapters of the present book reflect the organization of the conference. It opens with the "response" to *Address* by John Cage, which was the opening event of the conference and a work specifically conceived by Cage as such. (The nature of the event is described at the head of Chapter I.) The following chapters consist of most of the papers read at the five conference sessions, edited for publication, and some of the discussions among panelists and audience members that followed the papers, edited from transcripts of the tape-recorded sessions.

Acknowledgments

The conference on THE PHONOGRAPH AND OUR MUSICAL LIFE, directed by the present editor and Rita H. Mead, was made possible by a grant from the National Endowment for the Humanities, which also supported the recording and transcribing of the conference sessions. Other contributors to the conference included *Stereo Review,* through its editor William Anderson, and Brooklyn College, through its president at the time, John W. Kneller; the dean of its School of Performing Arts at the time, Robert Hickok; and the chairman of its Department of Music, Dorothy Klotzman.

Not susceptible to inclusion in the present book, for obvious reasons, were the public performances in lecture-recitals and demonstrations based on recordings of Joan Morris, soprano, and William

Bolcom, pianist; Henry Pleasants; and Carolyn Rabson. Technical assistance in recording the conference sessions was provided by Conrad Cummings and Laura Owens. Raw transcripts of the from-the-floor discussions were typed by Nancy Pardo and Frances Solomon, of the I.S.A.M. staff; Ms. Solomon, I.B.M. Composer operator extraordinary, typed the camera-ready copy for this book. Along the way, helpful criticism of the text was provided by Ruth Hilton (New York University), Richard Wentworth (University of Illinois Press), and Claire Brook (W. W. Norton and Company).

The greatest contributions of all, however, were those of the participants in the conference, who speak in the pages that follow (and are identified in the Appendix). To them the present editor dedicates his share of the book (without, however, relinquishing his own responsibility for any errors of commission, omission, or interpretation that his sometimes strenuous editorial hand has introduced in it).

H. W. H.
December 1979

I

"RESPONSE" TO *ADDRESS* BY JOHN CAGE

The first event of THE PHONOGRAPH AND OUR MUSICAL LIFE consisted basically of a new work by John Cage called Address, *which itself was made up of two pieces presented simultaneously. One of these,* 33-1/3 *(1969), called for a large number of phonograph systems (each with its own loudspeakers, pile of recordings available, and an "attendant" to lend any necessary assistance) deployed around the perimeter of the large backstage area of Whitman Auditorium, a 2300-seat concert hall at Brooklyn College. There were no seats backstage. The audience for* 33-1/3 *soon realized that they were the performers, too, and could play any of the available records on the phonograph tables. The other piece, conceived by Cage for the occasion, was titled* Cassette. *It called for a conference table (at one side of the backstage area) heaped with pre-recorded cassette tapes and five cassette playback systems (each with its own speakers), with five persons seated behind the table to play the cassettes* ad libitum.

Members of the audience for Address *entered the auditorium from its foyer and had to wind their way through the empty, dark hall to reach, finally, the backstage area by a side door. Their path led them through—literally—three spotlighted chamber ensembles, widely separated from each other. Each ensemble was playing (and continued to play throughout* Address*) a different one of Erik Satie's pieces of* musique d'ameublement: *"Tapisserie en fer forgé—Pour l'arrivée des invités (grande réception)—à jouer dans un vestibule," "Musique d'ameublement (Tenture de Cabinet préfectoral)," and "Carrelage phonique (peut se jouer à un lunch ou à un contrat de mariage)."*

The hundreds of records piled on the phonograph-system tables had been chosen at random from the Brooklyn College Music Library's collection. The pre-recorded cassettes on the conference table were all of addresses, lectures, or readings; they had been taped by Cage himself, by Buckminster Fuller, by Norman O. Brown, and by members of the Cassette *panel. The subjects of the recorded talks were very diverse.*

By Cage's design, Address *lasted for the length of a conventional academic address—about forty-five minutes. Its conclusion was signaled by the ringing of an electric bell (like that with which an academic institution announces the end of class periods). Thereupon chairs were provided for the audience, the "performers" of* Cassette *remained behind the conference table (but now in the role of panelists), and the following "Response" to Cage's* Address *ensued.*

CHARLES HAMM: I think it might be interesting if we begin by hearing a bit about the genesis of the composition we just participated in.

WILEY HITCHCOCK: When we decided to hold this conference, we thought about various people who might be appropriate to give an opening address, a sort of keynote speech. Among others, the name of John Cage came to mind, so I wrote to him and asked if he would be interested. He wrote me back very quickly: "I should be very much interested. Unfortunately, I am going to be in Cologne on December 7th. However, I could prepare a work that would be in effect a recorded address—if that would not be too appropriate." So what we've all helped to do here is create John Cage's newest work—*Address*, incorporating *33-1/3* (the work involving record playback systems) and a brand-new work, *Cassette* (involving cassette decks and their own speaker systems). I was sure, and John Cage agreed, that, since there would be many reactions to *Address*, it seemed sensible to set up some kind of situation where we could all respond to the experience. Hence, a "response" to the "address."

The people who were the performers of *Cassette* and who are now sitting here as a panel are the chairpersons of the forthcoming "formal" sessions of the conference: Richard Crawford, Stoddard Lincoln, Vivian Perlis, and myself. Joshua Rifkin, the other chairperson-to-come, had airplane trouble, so Charles Amirkhanian is sitting in for him. Charles Hamm is here as chairperson of this "Response" because of an essay he wrote titled "Technology and Music: The Effect of the Phonograph."[1] That essay gave me the idea of convening a group of people of varied interests in the field of music to talk about the impact on our musical culture of the phonograph and recorded sound in general. So it seemed only right to give Charles the honor, if you will, of moderating this opening panel.

HAMM: Thank you. . . . Let me make a few comments on what has just happened here, and invite all of you to do the same. Coming down from Dartmouth College on Air New England, to get my mind off the way the plane was pitching and the uncertainties of landing I began thinking of possible topics for discussion. I came up with titles like "The Phonograph as Mother" and "The Phonograph as Butcher Knife." These were intended to be provocative. But the first one I thought of was "The Phonograph as Photograph."

There is a certain similarity between the invention of the phonograph and the invention of the photograph. They did not happen at the same time, of course: the photograph was invented some decades before the phonograph. But you can make a case that the two had similar impacts on the fields of art and music. Both fixed something that had been impossible to fix before: the photograph made it possible to fix a very realistic scene, and the phonograph a sound (at first not very realistically, but increasingly so), in such a way that it was there whenever you wanted to refer to it. Not surprisingly, I think, the early periods of both the photograph and the phonograph saw them used as extensions of art and music as they had been up to that time. Photographers did portraits, landscapes, and dramatic scenes; their photographs can be, and have been, exhibited in the same museums as paintings. Thus, at first, the photograph did not create something entirely new. Likewise, the phonograph did not create something new; it was simply a way of dealing with something that was already there. In fact, for most of its existence the phonograph has functioned as a substitute for a concert: it has simply made it possible for people to hear music—the same music as before, but in different circumstances.

More interesting, I think, is the fact that a few people in the history of the photograph, and particularly in the twentieth century, took a somewhat different view of it: rather than thinking of the camera as a means of extending what had already been done in art, they began doing things impossible to do in art. The same thing has happened, of course, with the phonograph. A few people have seen the phonograph as a new medium and as a means, not of simply putting into another form what we already have but of creating something new. Obviously, that is what John Cage has done tonight, as he has in many other pieces. The first time that he did this was in *Imaginary Landscape No. 1*, of 1939. That is a work in which he used two variable-speed turntables to create as part of the compo-

[1]Charles Hamm, Bruno Nettl, and Ronald Byrnside, *Contemporary Music and Music Cultures* (Englewood Cliffs: Prentice-Hall, Inc., 1975), chapter 9.

sition a sound that had not been possible before. In fact, one thread running through Cage's career as a composer has been the use of the phonograph and other electronic equipment, not to reproduce sound but to create sound—to bring about something that could not exist otherwise. And that, of course, is exactly what happened tonight.

RICHARD CRAWFORD: One thing that struck me about tonight's experience was that, although recorded sound was a big part of what was being heard, a recording of the whole event would be catastrophic. The experience that occurred is over, and I don't know if anyone would want to re-create it. The work seems to have been a slice of unreproduceable experience.

HAMM: And therefore it was anti-phonograph, it seems to me. Let me try to explain that by going back to my earlier analogy:

I'm not sure it could be proved, but I think that once the photograph was developed some artists, at least, were forced to think, "There is no point in my trying to paint absolutely realistic things, because we can now do that by other means. So what can art do that the photograph cannot do?" Of course, many artists had thought along such lines before there ever was such a thing as a photograph. But I would guess that at least some of the things that happened in the late nineteenth and early twentieth centuries in art were a reaction against the photograph, or a recognition of what in a sense it had freed the artist to do. I see a parallel with the phonograph: from the point of view of the composer, the phonograph can be considered as something which merely reproduces what can be produced in other ways—a symphony, a string quartet, and so forth. Potentially, the phonograph is destructive of live music; it hasn't worked out wholly that way, but the danger is there. And some composers have begun thinking, "What can we do in music that cannot be captured on the phonograph and that will therefore still be valid even though we have the phonograph?" This relates to what Mr. Crawford said, because, true, Cage's *Address* could not be captured on a single recording.

CHARLES AMIRKHANIAN: I'd like to react to that, and to Richard Crawford's comments. Having been present at the first performance of *33-1/3*—and, in fact, having recorded it in four-channel sound for radio broadcast—I can say that this was a *superb* performance tonight. The clarity of sound in this space here was really tremendous. Also, a very interesting social thing happened, with people getting together and talking and hearing the speech of others, and then hearing the recordings and tapes intrude. I think that if more of us had shut our eyes we would have heard something wonderful. Also, walking through the Satie music was a terrific experience; that was very nicely done, from the theatrical standpoint. In short, it was a very nice experience and, contrary to Mr. Crawford, I would *like* to have a recording of it—a good recording, on a Nagra machine, in stereophonic sound.

RITA MEAD: Your comment about the social aspect of this experience is important. If we had not had all that sound going on as we came in, we would all have sat down in chairs very quietly, and listened, and then waited for the panel to talk. Instead, there was so much sound we could not take it all in, and instead we used it as background and then started talking to all the people around us, and having a marvelous time. So, we have started a conference on the phonograph by ignoring it! Certainly it seems to me that Cage was making some comment by creating this experience for us. He hates the phonograph, began hating it in school when he had to identify musical selections played on one, but he has created something with it.

DICK HIGGINS: I'd like to make a comment in another area, that of poetry. I notice a structural difference when texts are made to be recorded. Normally, when a poet makes a text, it's intended to be heard just once through, in the course of a poetry reading or something of that sort. A difference exists when poems are meant to be recorded, because the things the poet has in mind will exist, say, while driving through traffic with the poem being played on a cassette in the car, or, if it's on a record, the poem will be played not just once but repeatedly—perhaps to teach a course in English or some other kind of study. The recording process has changed the situation physically, and it's changed how the poet thinks of the work's being experienced; something structurally different has happened in the sensibility of the language. The poet now is not orienting himself towards "I'll wipe them out at my reading"; he considers that he is instead going to create words as a sort of environment. Poetry no longer has the apocalyptic element, I think, as a result of this; that ended with "beat" poetry back in the 1950s. For the last twenty years poetry has become more and more environmental and situational, partly as a result of the phonograph and now, even more, of cassettes. Any number of companies are using them; there's even a magazine of poetry on cassettes, called *Black Box.*

CRAWFORD: I'd like to say something from the performer's standpoint, having been one tonight. It was interesting how, without planning any strategy, we performers of *Cassette* gradually developed a slightly competitive point of view. I started off with what I thought was a fairly discreet low volume-level, not wanting to be too assertive right off the bat. But then, as other sounds gradually began to impinge on my cassette, I jacked up the level a little. Then things got fairly cacophonous, and I found myself watching each of the other cassette "stations," and when another player would change a cassette, or when I could tell that a certain loud portion was about to stop, I would quickly rev mine up. At the same time, I found that others had caught on (or maybe they were already way ahead of me) and seemed to be following the same strategy. But then, when Charles Hamm arrived, a bit late, it was a whole new ball game: he came in, turned on his cassette very loud, and then sat and read his program. That wiped me out.

VIVIAN PERLIS: That relates to Dick Higgins's comments about poetry and recordings. Those of us who play records or tapes have a certain kind of power. Conversely, a poet loses some of his power if his poem is recorded and can be "played" by any number of people in any place they want, combined with whatever they want.

HARRY SALTZMAN: I think there's an interesting contrast between what you people on the panel could do with the cassettes and what one could do with earlier Cage pieces—for instance, *Imaginary Landscape No. 4,* for radios, in which the performers (I happen to know, having once played concert radio) can alter what is happening as in any other kind of music: changing the amplitude and the frequency, making musical connections, and so forth. Really, it's very close to conducting or playing a musical instrument. It's a very *human* experience. But, as suggested by Richard Crawford's description, you people could only turn up the volume; there was really very little you could do . . .

CRAWFORD: We could turn the volume *down,* too!

SALTZMAN: . . . and so what I would call the "inhuman" or "non-human" aspects that recordings lend to the musical experience were brought out in this piece. I think there's a very big difference, in other words, between Cage's earlier piece and this one.

AUDIENCE MEMBER: Related to what Mr. Saltzman said about the "inhumanness" of recorded music, the record industry has been making records so perfect by technology and editing that you lose any sense of the fallibility of humans. Such recordings are a fiction: they're too perfect, so when you go to a concert you are almost let down by what you hear.

WILLIAM MCCLELLAN: Whether perfect, pluperfect, or imperfect, any recording is a distortion of reality, just as a newsreel is a distortion of a news event. A recording is a distortion of an actual performance.

AUDIENCE MEMBER: I tend to disagree with that. The question is: what's the real thing and what is not? I recently heard a recording of a performance I had attended, and I thought, "My God! It sounds far better than it was! How did it happen? I was there!"

HAMM: You can get into great complexities there. Take the harpsichord, for example. What is a good recording of a harpsichord? Some recordings have been made with the mike so close to the instrument that you hear things that you would never hear "live," even in a small room. Many people who get to know the harpsichord from recordings go to a recital and are very much disappointed: they can hardly hear the instrument. They have heard "unrealistic" harpsichord sounds on recordings–but what is real? And there are recordings of rock and folk music in which you can hear the guitar players' fingers actually sliding from one fret to another. You tend not to hear that in a live performance, but it brings you very close to the music. In that sense, maybe the recording is better than a live performance. On the other hand, we can all cite examples of performances in which things happened that would never emerge from a recording.

AUDIENCE MEMBER: I don't think that it's a qualitative matter; I don't think that the word "better" should be used. I don't think that a phonograph recording and a live performance should be in competition. Maybe they are, to some degree, but they are also independent entities.

HAMM: Getting back to tonight's experience: no one has made any comment about the combination of the Satie pieces, out there in the auditorium, and the Cage work, here backstage.

AUDIENCE MEMBER: My understanding is that Cage's work *Address* consists of *33-1/3* and the new work, *Cassette;* it's a combination. I'm not sure whether the Satie pieces were part of *Address* or, if not, what the relationship is.

HITCHCOCK: Cage is Cage; Satie is Satie. Their relationship is something else again.

AUDIENCE MEMBER: My reaction, as I walked through the hall and heard the different sounds of the Satie pieces coming at me, and walked through the players and then up here, and then talked with neighbors and walked across the room and heard this music and the speeches happening, with the different sounds seeming to move around as I did, was simply that it was amazing! Was John Cage's piece a mechanical conception of Satie's music? Were they supposed to do the same thing? Did they?

HAMM: Thank you. I've been hoping for some time that someone would try to make some connection between the works by the two composers.

PERLIS: I might hazard the suggestion that this experience could be viewed as a sample of what has happened to us in real life with all kinds of sound–recorded sound, live music, voices, machines. In perhaps emphasized form, our experience tonight is what has happened to us in our lives, and in our musical culture. I'm not sure that John Cage was intending to make a statement like that; I would not be surprised, however, if, as he usually does, he had some such idea, some aesthetic statement.

HITCHCOCK: I suppose *Address* is, as Charles Hamm has suggested, an anti-phonograph piece. But on the other hand, as Vivian suggests, it certainly is a kind of paradigm of a world saturated with phonc graphs, and with sounds all around us. In that sense, it is very much a piece of recorded sound, a piece that takes its very premises from the existence of recorded sound. This is an aspect of Cage that I think is interesting: he accepts the phonograph, and he has led us through live music, and then has built—wit the phonograph and with another species of sound reproduction, the cassette deck—the possibilities for an experience. He has laid it open for us and said, "Here, you take it!"—for about forty-five minutes, the length of a conference address.

II

THE PHONOGRAPH AND THE AUDIENCE

The first session of THE PHONOGRAPH AND OUR MUSICAL LIFE addressed itself to the effects that the phonograph and sound recording have had on "the audience" for music. The term was interpreted very broadly: not only do concertgoers make up the musical audience; so do people who listen by choice to music on radio and recordings, and people who, willy-nilly, hear strains of music through recorded "environmental-music" systems in restaurants, hotel lobbies and elevators, banks, and airplane cabins. The session was chaired by musicologist-pianist-arranger Joshua Rifkin and included as panelists a university undergraduate (Christopher Campbell), a foundation executive associated with the world of country music (William Ivey), a vice-president of the Muzak Corporation (Jane Jarvis), and an editor of a leading audio-equipment and recordings magazine (James Goodfriend).

William Ivey

RECORDINGS AND THE AUDIENCE FOR THE REGIONAL AND ETHNIC MUSICS OF THE UNITED STATES

We must recognize during this conference two different historical events. Certainly some of our remarks will relate directly to the wonderful *invention* of the phonograph one hundred years ago. My remarks will relate to the more recent discovery that music could be placed on cylinders or discs and that people would purchase these in quantity.

I, in fact, am interested in an even more subtle discovery: that the folk musics found in the United States could be recorded and that *these* records could be sold. I am interested in the long-term interaction between recordings and the music of geographical and ethnic communities, so my general remarks should be taken to apply primarily to this interaction.

It is important that we do not view the impact of recordings upon the audience for musical performance as an isolated phenomenon. It is only one portion of the total impact that technology has had upon the audience for all art during the past seventy-five years. Recordings have done to music what film and television have done to drama, and what photography has done to painting (though the precise effect here is somewhat different), and we should never be so unsophisticated as to elevate recordings to a unique place within the history of technological innovation. Technology brings certain things to art, and we have witnessed its effect for a sufficiently long time to have come to understand what some of these effects are.

We know that recording makes performances repeatable, and that it allows them to be spread across the land to a much larger audience than might have heard an original musical event. The performance can live forever; it can be drawn upon for education and inspiration far into the future.

This effect is presumably positive, for the good of the art, but others seem not so beneficial. Certainly recordings have increased the distance between performer and audience, and have decreased audience participation in the musical event. Recordings today have also, just as certainly, set near-perfect standards of excellence in performance, but standards which are often unfairly applied in a "live" context. In this sense at least, the tail of musical art is wagging the dog. Furthermore, these standards are national and dictate not only how music ought to be performed but also what styles are worth performing. We once had a fairly vigorous assortment of regional musical styles in this country in both popular and folk traditions, but the impact of recordings—setting national standards of what, and how, music should be performed—has pushed us toward a homogenization of these distinctive traditions. Local musicians now succeed or fail according to their ability to imitate precisely the sound of national hits. Under such pressure, local and regional styles have tended to vanish under a deluge of national styles.

This brings me to a related point, but one that is larger in its implications than those made above. It seems, on balance, that recordings are ultimately hostile to creativity. It has become a modern cliché to view the musician in the recording studio, slaving over miles of tape, as the perfect image of musical creativity. If creativity is seen as experiment or adventure, however, the perfection demanded of the recorded product appears incompatible with the sense of danger—of "going out on a limb"—that characterizes creative performance in many of our musics. I have heard many fans of country and popular music complain that an artist failed in a concert because he "didn't sound like the record." It would thus appear that even a star—someone presumably freed by success to create and experiment—is held prisoner by the demand of his audience that he sound like his studio product.

I want to restate what I've said in a slightly different way, lest you think I have strayed from our basic subject of "recordings and the audience." Recordings have, quite simply, changed the way we hear music. Performances are now joyously diffused through space and preserved through time, but our audience has come to focus excessively upon the recording itself rather than upon the music it contains. This kind of distinction has been made by many observers of technology and culture—by Marshall McCluhan, Daniel Boorstin, and others—but it remains worthwhile to stress again that our audience today is an audience for recordings rather than an audience for music. Musical standards are those of recordings, and these standards are applied by the audience to all music. The audience of today eschews local stylists in deference to national hits. The audience spurns creative experiment for the blander perfections of the recording studio. And the audience participates in our national mania for the technology which is, in theory, only supportive of art: thus, the modern listener is frequently described as an audiophile or a "hi-fi nut" or a "record nut," in proper semantic recognition of the diminished role of music in all of this.

Time plays an important role in the relationship between the audience and recordings. If we conceive of time as history, it is easy to discover a period in which recordings were subordinate to live performances of music. I am speaking in generalities here, but I think everyone would agree that wide dissemination of sheet music and folios in the days before recordings depended upon a network of amateur musicians and, therefore, upon an audience that was musically literate and geared toward performance. In the first few decades of disc recordings, they competed with live performances in sound quality, and they were usually found inferior to the live sound. During this same period, musical literacy remained an attribute of general education, and the habit of home performance from sheet music remained strong. But with the introduction of vinyl discs and the development of audio equipment capable of reproducing the full range of frequencies and approximating the dynamic range of live music, the need for musical literacy among the audience for music waned. Recordings became so demonstrably superior in sound to what could be produced by amateurs in the home that only the most determined families retained the "social music" tradition so prevalent in the nineteenth century.

Even for musicians—and we must never cease to regard musicians as an important part of the audience for recordings—the need for musical literacy was reduced, because performance techniques could be learned by ear, using the repeatability of recordings. During the past half-century, recordings have brought increasingly good sound into homes, but they have thereby undoubtedly removed some of the drive behind amateur musicianship. The audience for music has not only fallen prey to the standards of recorded music, but its involvement in music-making has been reduced by easy access to quality recordings. It may be true that, for the committed professional musician, recordings have opened new vistas of experience and education. The audience, however, is dumber than it used to be; modern Americans are better consumers of records than ever before, but they are poorer music-listeners.

The recording has come to dominate and determine the relationship between the average listener and music only recently, since the introduction of the long-playing vinyl disc. Any listener thirty years of age or younger has come of age musically in an era in which recordings have defined most of our contact with music. Time, and improvements in technology, have elevated recordings from pitiful imitations of reality to a new "super-reality" which confounds musicians intent on duplicating recorded material in a live setting.

Time is intertwined with the impact of recordings upon the music audience in ways other than through history. Certainly the recording has accelerated the pace of change within music, both the pace of stylistic change and the rapidity with which new faces replace old. I suspect that the world of classical music is somewhat immune to this trend, but certainly the vernacular forms—pop music, country music, and rhythm-and-blues—have fallen prey to the tendency of recorded music to "use up" styles, repertory, and people at a ferocious rate.

Country music, in the early days of commercial recordings, shared many characteristics with the Anglo-American folksong out of which it grew. The performance styles were archaic, unprofessional, and disinclined to rapid change. In fact, the twenty-year period between the early 1920s and the beginning of World War II is frequently lumped under the heading "Old Time" by country-music scholars. The term suggests stylistic consistency throughout this period, and there exists good evidence for such an attitude. On the other hand, the twenty years following the beginning of World War II witnessed the rise and decline of many styles of country music, as this basically folk-music form fell under the influence of the demand for fad which accompanied the spread of music on recordings at a rapid pace. Folk music is defined as music which is transmitted by ear, from person to person, face to face. The pace of stylistic change is slow in such oral tradition. One measure of the impact of recordings is seen in the fact that it took only twenty years to impose upon Southeastern folksong the appetite for change and innovation which characterizes popular music.

Recordings represent a rapid means of disseminating music, and of course recordings are, in a very real sense, marketed by AM and FM radio, which only adds to the speed of dissemination. The recording/radio complex has a healthy appetite for new musical styles, and it also consumes individual performers voraciously. In popular music, each singer has his or her day in the sun, and despite the intensity of popularity at one moment, a career can fade with surprising speed as the darling of one season is replaced with a new voice and face. The rapid turnover in the stars of popular music is so characteristic of the genre that only the exceptions—the Sinatras or the Presleys—are deemed worthy of comment. Country music was, at first, highly resistant to this tendency to consume and discard one performer after another. This resistance was predictable, because the folk music from which country music developed did not demand a rapid turnover of talent. On the contrary, a folk-singer remained in that position for life, once he had established a role within a community. Early commercial country entertainers drew upon this kind of loyalty from their audience. Roy Acuff, for example, first gained national exposure on record and radio in the late 1930s, but some of the fans he acquired in those days remain fans of his today; their devotion has remained constant over nearly forty years. Other country entertainers, such as Ernest Tubb and Hank Snow, have cultivated this kind of relationship with their fans—a relationship not unlike, in an earlier era, that between a folk-singer and his community. This kind of country-music fan does not demand that music continually astound or surprise him. He is, in fact, devoted to the unchanging nature of his favorite entertainers and prefers this steady quality to what he perceives as the fanciful exploits of popular music.

Country music is now, however, becoming part of the popular-music mainstream, and the forty-year stardom of Roy Acuff cannot be duplicated today. Blues and rhythm-and-blues—other folk-based forms of popular music—have experienced similar pressures as they have entered the pop mainstream. Howling Wolf or Muddy Waters have had the kind of long-term popularity that was shared by early country-music entertainers, but as their kinds of music have gained a larger and larger share of the popular-music audience, they too have been swept up by the pace of popular music, and this pace has made these styles and people disposable: "You're no hotter than your last record" is true not only for musicians, but for whole musics.

All of these problems, or at least most of them, can be attributed to the amount of recorded music available today. "Available" is perhaps not the right word. We are deluged with recorded music at every turn. It accompanies our driving and our shopping; it is heard in the background behind our work; and it "backs up" our meals at home. With this exposure, this immersion, in recorded music, it comes as little surprise that the audience is jaded, bored, and harder and harder to "reach." Music has taken on an almost utilitarian definition: it is *for* something—for relaxing, for stimulating, for dancing, for background. Music in such a context is always something subordinate, something supportive of a mood or activity. As we, the audience, grow more and more at home with music behind our daily routine, our ability to listen hard—to focus our every nerve upon a passage or phrase—has become diminished.

Technology has always been seductive, particularly to Americans, perhaps because our society has been responsible for so much technological innovation. We have learned, of course, that a technological solution is never an unmixed blessing. Certainly, contemporary concerns with the natural environment are in a large part a recognition that technology has carried a high price-tag. In the various fields of artistic endeavor, technology has not always had a beneficial impact. I am sure that recordings were once seen as the greatest boon to the world of music, for suddenly the world possessed the means to preserve and transmit great performances with ease. But the hidden effects—and perhaps the more important effects—of recordings upon music seem, however, to have been negative ones. The audience is more distant, less involved, less knowledgeable, perhaps less discerning than in the days when music was less available, less common, and less a part of our daily routine. The wonderful disc, which spread music through time and space, has itself become a barrier which limits our involvement and our perception. It has, perhaps, taken us this first hundred years to see the ambiguous character of this faithful servant of music. Perhaps we will not need another century to master fully this wonderful technology in a way which allows it to support and improve musical art.

JOSHUA RIFKIN: I would question one thing. You say that recordings can imprison artists, in that audiences expect them to sound like their records. But is this relationship really so different from the faithful-audience/artist relationship that you later describe with, let's say, performers like Roy Acuff and Ernest Tubb? Very often a performer's faithful audience over the years also wants a performer to do nothing new, nothing different.

WILLIAM IVEY: Perhaps that is an inconsistency in my argument. But when I speak of the prison of recordings, I am thinking of it as one of detail. That is, it really demands a rather massive technological effort to take that recording out on the road and duplicate it. Now, the kinds of fans of a Roy Acuff do not demand, and have never demanded, that he sound like his records. I think they're mainly interested in the event of having him present. That is the nature of their devotion: it's a personal loyalty, rather than a loyalty to his material.

JAMES GOODFRIEND: I think that basically what you've got with the audience for somebody like Roy Acuff is a familiarity with a personality and a style; exact duplication of phraseology and notes, in singing the same song four or five times, is not necessary.

AUDIENCE MEMBER: Yes, since the style of Acuff and many country singers is not perfect to begin with—they don't have perfect tone, perfect range, perfect pitch—so when they come to sing, it sounds just like the record; it isn't very different.

RIFKIN: And the records are not so elaborately produced. An Acuff performance is basically the same on record as a live performance, whereas the immense complication of certain rock productions cannot be duplicated live.

IVEY: That's a very important point. Had I thought of it, I would certainly have mentioned that there was an age in which the way you made records was simply to go in and play; you did not have at hand the kind of technology that allowed you to do anything different—not to say better—than you could do out on a stage. I think country music was characterized by this approach to recording until, really, the last five or ten years. Now, suddenly, country musicians are faced with having to act like a rock band when they go on the road: they have to take along two semi-trailer truckloads of speakers and sound technicians, because their audience is now beginning to place these new demands on them.

CHRISTOPHER CAMPBELL: One important part of the difference between a live and a recorded performance may be that in a lot of live performances (I can remember one of the Guarneri Quartet, and also some of rock bands) the kind of electricity that passes back and forth between the performers as they're working is something that is lacking in a studio. I was in the Columbia Records studios a couple of weeks ago, and some band, I guess it was the Blue Oyster Cult, was laying down tracks, but there was only one artist there. I said, "Where's the band?" and they said, "Well, he's the one we have today." There were twenty-four tracks on this huge tape, and they were laying down one track at a time; each guy would listen on earphones and add his particular contribution. So, the electricity I'm talking about will be totally lacking in *that* kind of final product.

RIFKIN: But I think all four of the Guarneri Quartet record at once!

GOODFRIEND: I'd like to make a distinction here among certain kinds of music, which I think will back up one of Mr. Ivey's points about people these days being very much more record fans and less music fans—that is, knowing more about records and less about music. I think the general audience today has an availability of repertoire that was totally unknown to music-listeners twenty years ago. The sheer quantity and variety of music that is known by the average person who has a phonograph today is just unbelievable. And yet, of course, he listens to it in a much more superficial way than the person twenty years ago did. The person twenty years ago had access to, say, fifty pieces of classical music. He got to know those fifty pieces quite well, because when he wanted to play records, that's what he played. If he didn't have records, he went to the concert hall, and there too he heard a relatively limited repertoire. But getting into a differentiation of musics here: with the advent of rock (and I think it's still very much a characteristic of rock), what was important was not the song. What is remembered in rock is a particular entity of music and technology, all put together in a very specific way and infinitely repeatable on the record, and *only* on the record.

RIFKIN: That might mean that rock is different from what we normally define as pop music—the song which retains its fundamental identity in spite of transformations—and has taken on a character that we associate more typically with composed music, with "serious" music.

GOODFRIEND: Right.

JANE JARVIS: Actually, rock has brought about a proliferation of music, and almost a homogenization of music. Because, as Mr. Ivey pointed out, there's practically no such thing as pure country music any more. It is there, but in very small quantities. From what I see in *Billboard* and other trade papers, country artists are including pop styles, and it's even affected hard-core folk music.

IVEY: Yes. This relates to the shrinking play-list of AM radio and the impact of rack-jobbing as the main technique for the distribution and sale of recordings. Those two things have had a great impact on the kinds of records that are made, because to be successful today a record must have the capability of getting a spot on the play-list of a radio station, and it must have the capability of selling well enoug so that a rack-jobber will pick it up. This is something completely apart from how it sounds, or who the artist is, or what the basic style is.

MARTIN WILLIAMS: I have a couple of slight reservations about your implications of "pure country style." Even the earliest recordings in that idiom showed the incorporation of black twelve-bar blues, and this was itself due to the influence of recordings. The early repertory, far before World War II, of groups like the Light Crust Doughboys, included jazz of the late twenties and the early thirties—not only the style but the tunes themselves. Bluegrass music is really a kind of country version of Dixieland, with different instruments (the string band instrumentation). So I think it's a mistake to call any of this "pure."

IVEY: I would agree with you to this extent: I myself hate to fall into the routine of saying that the pre-World War II stuff is the good old folky material, and everything since then is the nasty commercial material. This is a distinction that folklorists, in particular, have made for years, and a lot of what I do in my work is designed to defeat that. But I think the connection between blues and country, which is a very early one, is *not* one based on recordings; I think it's primarily based on actual face-to-face contact between musicians. I think that was in the folk tradition. I'll grant you, though, that Western swing—the Light Crust Doughboys, Bob Wills—because of their relationship with Southwestern fiddlers and their knowledge of Joe Venuti's violin style, may well have come about primarily from contact with records.

Jane Jarvis

NOTES ON MUZAK

I'd like to tell you what Muzak is today and I'd like then to tell you of the roots of Muzak.

Muzak is a company that provides functional music as a tool of management in environmental situations. We furnish music in work areas, primarily in offices and factories. We do furnish Muzak in a few other kinds of places—like stables, to keep horses calm—but our primary function is the furnishing of environmental music in work areas.

Now, I'm sure you're wondering, "What can she mean by 'environmental music'?" Muzak was the first company—and the only company, to my knowledge—to look upon music as a raw material to be sequentially programmed in such a way as to have an ever-rising stimulus curve. The theory was based on music's ability to combat fatigue. This was not an idea just taken out of thin air. Although Muzak had been doing some studies on its own, it was actually based on a study done by Wyatt and Langdon during World War II, for the British government. They were trying to determine whether music enhanced productivity in war plants, and their tests proved conclusively that the use of music in an ever-rising stimulus curve to combat fatigue was very desirable.

Based on that, Muzak did tests of its own, and we have subsequently been able to prove to the satisfaction of every major manufacturing company in the world that music provided by us and used in an environmental setting increases productivity. Now, we do not say that if you use Muzak in an office or a factory a lazy person is going to work harder. We do not say that it's going to make people come to work on time. We do not say that it will make them like their boss, or that they will not look forward to going home, or that they'll forfeit vacations or coffee breaks. We simply say that we provide an environmental situation of a euphoric nature that enhances productivity.

We provide three basic services: one is for offices, another is for light industry, and the other is for heavy industry. Heavy industry is defined as having a very high noise level in the work area. The music that we provide there is of a somewhat percussive and penetrating nature. An office, on the other hand, where there's very little shuffling of feet or very little traffic, perhaps only one typewriter and no business machines to speak of, does not require the same degree of penetration or stimulus to make its impact. Therefore, a different kind of music is provided for such a work area. The music we provide for light industry is somewhere half-way between.

Our standardized programs are made up of music which, I repeat, we consider raw material, sequentially programmed to produce a rising stimulus curve, in fifteen-minute segments. This is based on the fact that silence is as important a factor in music as the sound itself. You cannot react to music if you do not have an opportunity to respond; music that is dovetailed loses its effectiveness. Each of the fifteen-minute programs is an actual little program: it's carefully planned, with an opener and a closer, like any good program. The first selection in a program has the least stimulus, and each selection thereafter rises somewhat in stimulus.

Although programming in a rising curve is well known to almost all performing artists, the idea of the computerized assignment of a stimulus code to each selection was fostered and effected by Mr. U. V. Muscio, Muzak's present president. Each individual selection is tested and measured so that we know what its stimulus factor is, and it is coded as such. In fact, every selection in our library has a dossier, so to speak. Thus, although a piece of music is subject to random programming by a compute it will not appear at the "wrong" time in a program—unless, of course, I make a mistake (which I've been known to do) and accidentally give the wrong stimulus code to it.

Now, at the beginning of the work day—and we assume that most work days are eight-hour days- the first group of selections, although a complete little program in itself, is of the lowest stimulus in character. Each succeeding group rises somewhat. That is not to say that the second group starts where the first one left off: it overlaps it somewhat, in stimulus content.

Tests have proved that in the mid-morning and mid-afternoon a terrible ennui sets in, for one reason or another. This is what gave birth to the coffee break. We don't for a moment say that people should not have coffee breaks, but if they don't have time for a coffee break we do something for the workers ourselves: we provide a stimulus curve that rises considerably above a "normal" curve. For one hour the succession of fifteen-minute programs shows a general rise in stimulus. Then, past that one hour of stimulus, we recede somewhat—although not as far down as we were before this period of the "hype," so to speak—and this continues until the lunch hour.

In the mid-afternoon we also have a one-hour period of extreme stimulus, which helps the mid-afternoon fatigue and boredom that beset almost everyone who is at work. Then we continue on until the end of the work day.

Now, the reason why this has been so successful is that it doesn't matter whether one lives in Japan (where we have a very large franchise), or Argentina, or any other part of the world—we're all human beings, and although our work areas may differ we are all victims of the same problems of fatigue, boredom, and declining productivity while at work. And Muzak has found a way of combating and relieving these problems, through the use in work areas of environmental music.

That's what we are today.

The basic idea of Muzak was the brain child of Major-General Squire, who was a Signal Corps officer in the United States Army. In 1922 he came up with the notion that something like Muzak shoul be sent to homes—that it would be great for housewives. Radio was just barely started, and Major-General Squire went to a company in Cleveland with the notion of sending out music not by radio but ove power lines. His idea met with modest success, but it didn't have any real clarity of viewpoint, and it was only music on phonograph records that was sent into people's homes. There were a few subscriber but it wasn't a financial bonanza by any means.

In 1934 the idea was revived by a music company in New Jersey, which started what we now kn as Muzak. (Nobody, by the way, seems to know for sure where the name came from.) The company transmitted in New York on direct power lines, originally just to hotel dining rooms and restaurants. At that point they weren't absolutely certain of their format, but somebody thought it would be a good idea to have marches for breakfast and pipe-organ music for lunch. In between they played classical music.

The company was then bought by Senator William Benton, who was also one of the founders of the Encyclopaedia Britannica. At that point it became pretty much what it is now. They began to record for themselves, since they couldn't find a pre-recorded product that seemed to suit what they were trying to do. The first orchestra to be recorded by Muzak was that of Sam Lannon, the brother of Lester Lannon. The second band to be recorded was Russ Morgan's, a very famous dance band of the Midwest. They used such a roster of stars it's really fun to think about it. Fats Waller recorded for Muzak, and so did Teddy Wilson, who was in the original Benny Goodman Sextet.

The first musical director of the company was Ben Selwyn, who stayed with Muzak for many years. His concept of the ideal sound was that of the hotel orchestra, and it was under his direction that the company ceased recording organized bands and began to go with orchestras that it formed itself and recorded under the baton of Ben Selwyn. (And curiously, although those early recordings were made with only one microphone, the engineers did a remarkable job of capturing the total sound of the music.)

At some point about 1953, it dawned on the corporate body that theirs was really a unique company and called for unique thinking. So they decided that the musical arrangements should not be stock arrangements but special ones, and, even if not copyrighted, not to be used by anybody else. Now, there's one unique thing about a Muzak arrangement—it was true then and it is true now, although the arrangements have changed in content because music has changed and recording technology has changed—and that is that it is a total entity. It is a great deal like a short story or even a novel: it has an introduction or an exposition; it has a theme and development of it; it has a climax, a denouement, and a closing. There's no such thing as a "fade" ending at Muzak, partly because in order to program a piece it has to have an opening and a close, in order to be able to assign it a stimulus code.

I could go on much longer, but rather than say anything more I'll wait to hear from you: I can tell I'm going to have a lot of questions.

WILLIAM IVEY: By "penetration" do you mean loudness?

JANE JARVIS: No, penetration depends on the nature of the instruments used and their manner of use—their percussiveness and the number of impulses and accents within the arrangement. The decibel level is another matter; that is determined by the sound engineers when they make an installation, the main principle being not to try to overcome noise: the sound level of Muzak should never be as high as the noise level in the room.

IVEY: Do you find that, depending on the ethnic composition of a factory work-force, you have to change the program content of the music you draw upon, or do you consider music as being culturally universal?

JARVIS: We deal with it as a cultural universal. Also, remember that we don't really care to raise anyone's awareness of the music.

MARGARET JORY: I wonder whether the existence of a captive audience like that of Muzak, which has become larger through the years—an audience that has become more and more used to doing something other than *listening* while music is playing—has changed the expectations not only for records but for live concerts. I wonder whether it has, in fact, affected the kind of music that is recorded and the duration of music that is recorded. If so, I wonder whether that's a healthy thing or whether it's not a healthy thing, and whether it should be combatted or encouraged.

JARVIS: I wonder which question I should answer. Are you asking whether there should be music at all?

JORY: No, no. I've been involved with programming live performances for a long time, and I've often wondered what an audience expects and why. One of my questions is this: if people are subjected to music regularly—eight hours a day—and are told basically not to listen to it because they are doing something else, are they then going to be capable of listening to music with concentration? I believe very much in *music*; I'm not sure that I believe in Muzak. I understand that hens may lay more eggs when you play music to them, and people probably produce more words, or whatever they're supposed to produce, but I'm not sure it's a healthy thing for music. I'd like to hear specifically how you feel it has affected the audience.

JARVIS: Obviously, it hasn't stemmed the flow of the purchase of music: the record-buying public was never greater. If anything, I'm inclined to think that the people who have been exposed to Muzak are probably a great deal more catholic in their views. If you are opinionated about music, you're likel to buy only the thing you like, but if you are exposed to every kind of music—which Muzak does, you see; it's not just Latin, or country, or rock, or folk, it's all of them—then you have a broader view.

ROGER REYNOLDS: For me, the essential distinction that needs to be made is the one between the active experience of listening and making discriminations, and the passive experience of hearing indiscriminately. I must say that I've had the thrilling and rare experience this morning of being *certain* about something: I am certain that Muzak is the single most reprehensible and destructive phenomenon in the history of music, precisely because it conditions the lack of discrimination, the lack of listening, in favor of the passive acceptance of hearing. This raises Muzak, in my estimation, even above the pernicious aspects of secondary and primary music education.

JARVIS: You must know that I don't agree with you at all, but I have to say that it was eloquently put. I think, somehow or other, I've failed to make one point, which is that as a musician you cancel yourself out as a consumer. As an analyst of music, as a purveyor of music, as a composer, you can't possibly appreciate the consumer, because your whole view of music is totally different. Remember that people who work in offices are not professional musicians. The Muzak that they are exposed to is a part of the environment. It's like a pretty painting, or the room decoration. We do not try to improve anybody's mind, we do not elevate, we do not cure anything. We are not a therapy; we are an environmental tool of management, and psychologically and physiologically successful because of the testing that we have done. But we definitely don't affect anybody's taste.

AUDIENCE MEMBER: Do you have any idea how many people listen to Muzak . . . and/or are subjected to it?

JARVIS: It's a staggering number, something like twenty-five million. You see, Muzak transmits twenty-four hours a day throughout the world.

CHARLES DODGE: Can you give us some notion of how you assign the stimulus codes? How do you test and measure them—by galvanic skin response, or what?

JARVIS: That's a good question, but it is very different from your first question. Muzak looks upon music from a totally musical point of view. In other words, we listen or study the score and we observe all sorts of things: the melody line; the number of musicians involved (it makes a difference whether there are four musicians or sixty); the instrumentation; the placement of the musicians at the time of the recording; the content of the arrangement; the personality and style of the arranger (we proved the difference between arrangers by actually recording the same tune arranged by two different arrangers); the use of the instruments; the percussiveness; the impulses; the pulse; the accent; the tempo; the rhythm. . . . Have I forgotten anything?

JAMES GOODFRIEND: Who do you measure it on? That's the question.

JARVIS: We have a regular legende that we use.

JOSHUA RIFKIN: A what?

JARVIS: L-e-g-e-n-d-e.

AUDIENCE MEMBER: I think the basic question is whether the staff determines these things, or whether there are people on whom the music is tested before it's released over the Muzak system.

JARVIS: Oh no, we don't have to test in that way, because everybody's reaction to a singular selection is different.

RIFKIN: Yes, but how do you measure? What is your test sample?

JARVIS: We have parameters, just like anybody.

RIFKIN: But who are the listeners whom you measure?

JARVIS: We do not measure the listeners. You're asking a musical question. This is a psychological question, and that is another matter.

CHRISTOPHER CAMPBELL: Is there one person whom you assign to listen to all these selections to give you a numerical rating?

JARVIS: One person? By all means, no. In fact, any one of you—I'm sure you're all musicians or you wouldn't be here—could be trained to do this.

RIFKIN: But it is someone within the corporation who listens to the selection and evaluates it.

JARVIS: Yes, according to parameters. And, as I said before, occasionally we make mistakes, and we give a selection a grade that it should not have.

AUDIENCE MEMBER: How do you know when you make a mistake? What tells you? Was it those people at the breakfast table when they were getting marches?

JARVIS: Well, let me put it this way: if you're supposed to have an ever-rising curve of stimulus and, all of a sudden, right out of nowhere, a selection comes into someone's stream of consciousness and they *hear* it, then you know it's out of place.

RIFKIN: But the question is: is the "they" who hear it and realize that it's out of place you—Jane Jarvis—or somebody in the Muzak organization, or somebody out in the plant who drops a bolt into the works?—somebody who says, "That music's wrong!"

JARVIS: It's all of those things. Every once in a while we get a phone call, and the caller will say, "Take that terrible tune out of the system!" And we listen to find out what went wrong, and it's always because it's been mis-programmed.

RIFKIN: In other words, something goes wrong and you try to evaluate it.

IVEY: I don't know how valuable it is for us to kick Muzak around any more. It seems to me that one of the options that disc and tape recording opened up to the world was the ability to make purely utilitarian uses of musical material. And I don't think there are vast differences in kind between AM radio programming, Muzak, much of the scoring that goes on behind television dramatic productions, and so on. These are utilitarian uses of music which may be high or low in our estimation, but it seems to me that they're somewhat outside the thrust of most of our concerns. I don't know that it's worthwhile to attack them any more.

MARTIN WILLIAMS: I personally have a negative reaction to Muzak or its equivalent. When I hear it, I cringe. I do not want music put to that use; I'm offended by it. I don't even want to be in the elevator to get to the third floor with it going on. However, I am equally offended by all of the upper-middle-brow people I know who put on Mozart or Bud Powell or Art Tatum, or whoever, and use *them* like Muzak.

JARVIS: The reason why classical music is so precious is that it is made to be listened to, and so is jaz They are not background music; they are not functional music. Therefore, you cannot possibly compare Muzak to classical music, or to jazz, or to any other music form as such.

ALLAN MILLER: I detect a pernicious compromise here, when Miss Jarvis tries to maintain a distinction between music that you listen to and music that you *don't* listen to. I think it's precisely Mr. Reynolds's point, and perhaps Mr. Williams's, too, that we are so trained by Muzak and its allies to have music around us that we don't listen to that we have produced a polluted society which has lost the ability to listen to music. If you have music around you all the time and never listen to it, you'll never learn how to listen when you want to.

JARVIS: You all seem to fail to recognize who you are. You're not ordinary people; you're all skilled people, people immersed in music.

MILLER: We're just unlobotomized!

James Goodfriend

THE PHONOGRAPH AND THE AUDIENCE

The first question to entertain is whether or not the phonograph—or, perhaps more properly, the phonograph record—*has* an audience or not. An audience, according to the dictionary, is an assembly of hearers. You, for example, are an audience, for you are an assembly of hearers. That is to say that you, apparently of your own free will, have elected to come here to subject yourselves to a discussion of the phonograph and the audience. You may be surprised at what you hear, but you come without the expectation of surprise and, on the other hand, with an expectation, probably essentially correct, as to what you *will* hear. In other words, you are an audience because you have informed yourselves of a forthcoming event, know enough about it to decide whether or not you want to attend it, and have elected to assemble and hear it.

Now, of course, people need not assemble physically to constitute an audience. Writers sometimes have audiences. That is to say, there may be a group of people who are familiar enough with the work of a specific writer so that they manage to inform themselves of the appearance of a new book by that writer and contrive to beg, borrow, or steal it for the purpose of reading it.

The factor underlying both of these sorts of audiences is a certain sophistication. In both cases the audience has some idea, possibly based on previous experience, of what to expect, and has decided to test that expectation to see if a desired satisfaction results.

Can phonograph records be said to have an audience in that sense? Well, in certain ways, yes. Miss Olivia Newton-John might be said to have an audience in that sense. Some people have heard her previous records, liked them, and are willing to bet that they will like her next record, and the one after that. That, certainly, is an audience. Beethoven has an audience, too, though it may be smaller than Miss Newton-John's. It works a little differently there, since Beethoven himself is not about to come out with any new records. But there is a certain small group of people, with new people constantly being added, that has listened to certain works of Beethoven and has made the decision that, having liked those, they will probably like others by the same composer. I would like to point out, however, that just as not all the people who buy records by Olivia Newton-John do so out of a deliberate decision based on experience of her earlier records, so not all the people who buy records of Beethoven's music do so on the basis that they have liked what they have heard of him before and are willing to go further. As a matter of fact, with Beethoven the number, or even the percentage, who buy out of sophistication is probably far smaller than with Miss Newton-John. If that were not the case, then we could legitimately expect, over a period of years, a relative equality of sales among all, or most, of Beethoven's recorded works—since the sophisticated audience would go, logically, from one work to another until there was nothing left to explore, and that is obviously not so. They could, of course, go until they hit a Beethoven work they *didn't* like, or perhaps two or three in a row they didn't like, and then they might conclude, again quite logically, that they were not an audience for Beethoven but an audience for certain works of Beethoven and not others. This is probably true, but it would, I think, account for only a part of the disparity between the popularity of, say, the Symphony No. 5 on the one hand and the A Minor Quartet, Op. 132, on the other. The rest of the disparity comes, I think, because there are people buying records of Beethoven who do not do it because they are an audience for Beethoven—that is, because they have sufficient sophistication to know what to expect and sufficient desire to test the expectation—but for other reasons.

At this point I would like to suggest that there is another way to classify those people who consume phonograph records and whom we might like to think of as an audience. That is, as a *market,* or as many different markets. A market is not described on the basis of how sophisticated it is or how it decides whether to be interested in something or not. A market is described only on the basis of *what* it buys, and how much. What a market buys is product. It may be an Olivia Newton-John product or a Beethoven product, art songs or dirty songs; it is just product. It is much easier to "read" a market than to "read" an audience. It is also more profitable.

Before I get into these overlapping categories any further, I would like to digress a moment and bring up the matter of who makes records and why. The "who" is relatively easy. Records are made by performers (solo, ensemble, orchestral, or choral, or mixtures thereof), by composers to a certain extent, by record companies as a whole, by a & r men, producers, and recording engineers. *Why* records are made is even simpler. Records are made mostly for two reasons: money or ego-satisfaction, or mixtures of the two. It has been said that records are also made out of charity, guilt, the desire for prestige, or for the public good, but these are all really forms of ego-satisfaction or, indirectly, money.

Of all the people or organizations whose motives are involved in the production of records, the attitude of the record company itself, or that of the man who determines what the corporate attitude will be, is the most important. For here there are certain clearcut differences between records that are produced from the different motivations. In general, those records that are produced largely out of ego-satisfaction tend to be produced for audiences, however small, while those records that are produced primarily for their potential sales are being produced for markets. I'd like to offer you a few examples of both of these.

There is a company on the West Coast called Genesis, which is essentially a one-man company. Genesis is a repertoire-oriented company; that is, Mr. Commagere, who owns and runs the company, looks for the repertoire that will interest him, finds artists who are willing to perform it, and records it. When I asked him once about possibly investigating what repertoires people might be interested in buying, he confessed that he had never given that matter any thought whatsoever.

A second company, Connoisseur Society in New York, is largely an artist-oriented company. The man who runs it, Alan Silver, finds artists who impress him and interest him. He also finds certain repertoire that interests him, but basically the repertoire is what the artists decide upon. Connoisseur Society has a certain cognizance of the market, but when a choice arises between whether they should do something for artistry or not do it because of the market, the artistry almost invariably wins. Connoisseur Society is almost always willing to duplicate repertoire on their own label, which is very dangerous for a small company, but they do it because they think the artist is important.

A third example: Everest Records, out on the West Coast. Everest has a repertoire that is based entirely on what *might* sell and what is available for leasing, since they rarely make their own records. The man who runs Everest, Bernard Solomon, has an absolutely incredible knack for finding early tapes made by artists who are just about to make it big on another label, and so he manages to get in on their coat-tails. So far as classical music is concerned, his is the best coat-tail company in the business.

A fourth example: RCA. This, obviously, is the only large company I have mentioned. RCA have stated a number of times that they will not record anything for which they cannot project a sale of 25,000 copies or more. RCA does comparatively little for prestige—that is, for ego-satisfaction. I have to emphasize, however, that their records are not necessarily inferior because of that. In general records produced for money are not necessarily inferior to those produced for ego-satisfaction. RCA has money, they have big artists, and they can do large projects, which these other companies cannot.

Now, to get back to my prior discussion: how do we know that what is out there is more of a market than an audience, or at least is seen that way? Well, the quantity of repertoire that is available for sale these days is so vast that no one can possibly comprehend it. No curious listener can say, "I liked the last piece of Classic-era music (or Renaissance music, or High Baroque music) I heard on records; I think I'll try the next." "The next" is almost infinite in number. It's even difficult for the listener to say that he liked the last Beethoven piano concerto and therefore would like to try the next, because, although there are only five of them plus an early piece, the different recordings of them available constitute an absolute maze, and one can't be familiar with them all.

How do we know this? Because the over-all sales figures from one piece to another related one are so totally different. The man who likes Beethoven's Fifth Symphony may never even get to hear the Fourth. We know it because companies do not advertise repertoire in this way. At best they may say, "You liked Colin Davis's recording of Sibelius's Second Symphony. Now you should buy Colin Davis's recording of the Fourth Symphony." That might imply a Colin Davis audience. To a certain extent there must be one. But more often, people look for advice. They may ask (since they liked the Sibelius Second by Davis) whether they will also like the Fourth by him. Or whether they will like it better by someone else. Or whether they will like it at all, no matter who does it. People are continually asking for advice. They do not want general advice (such as "Explore the Mozart piano concertos" or "Listen to some records by Arturo Benedetti Michelangeli"). They want to know which particular record they should buy. Most buyers see no relation between one record and another. They want single recommendations, and, in one way or another, all record selling is devoted to selling the single package (whether of one, two, or twelve records) which is in market competition with all other single packages. This is basically uninformed buying and uninformative selling, because the quality of the record is beside the point. That is only a selling tool. Even the repertoire is only a selling tool.

Over the years certain single packages have been found to sell better than others. Rimsky-Korsakov's *Scheherazade,* for one, considered as a product, sells very well, and every time someone makes a new one, it sells; Tchaikovsky's *1812 Overture,* for another; and so on. If there is an *audience* for either of these works, it must be a very small audience indeed. But the *market* for them is, in classical-music terms at least, enormous. Record companies will use any and every device in the world to establish a market, to search for a hidden market, to discover not a real need or a real desire but a point of sale, a record idea that can pierce the buyer's defensive armor and make him buy this record rather than another one.

This is less so in the non-classical fields, for people there, even if perhaps they know less about music, know more what they like—or at least what they want to be seen with. With younger people, peer pressure plays a terrific part in record sales. They are the most manipulatable market, for if they hear it continually on the radio, they know automatically that they must have it. (All but the smartest of them: the smart ones hear it the first time on the radio, decide for themselves whether or not they like it, and then call the station to tell them so, thus telling the manipulators which product to manipulate.) Older generations have more set tastes. They know the musical styles and the artists they like, and that is what they buy—up to a point. A pop buyer who has gotten married and has two children and a mortgage on the house ceases to be a factor in the market, for the most part—or even a part of the audience, except in the passive way of listening to radio or TV—because he stops buying records.

The jazz buyer is much more like the classical buyer, except that, more than the classical buyer, he gen erally knows what he is going to like before he hears it.

To get back to the classical market and the classical audience:

We have this rather large classical market—on which, by the way, the classical record industry de pends for its very existence. (A small percentage up and we are in years of plenty. A small percentage down and small companies go bankrupt while large ones talk of discontinuing their classical lines altogether.) And we have a number of really quite tiny classical audiences—that is, those buyers who have both the sophistication and the desire in a certain small field of music, one that *can* be encompas The largest of these is the opera audience. Opera buyers are often looked upon as freak buyers becaus of their exclusive tastes, but they are no more freakish than other specialized buyers; it's only that the are many more of them, so they are more visible. Intelligent record companies play to this audience through the continued use of favorite artists in favorite works, but also with an eye toward expanding the commercially viable operatic repertoire. A new recording of an obscure Verdi opera, for example, probably has a better chance of making a profit than a first recording of many a better-known sympho The opera audience behaves like an audience. That is, it investigates, keeps itself informed, and makes buying decisions based on thought-out expectations. Needless to say, this audience does not account for all the sales of opera records, but it forms a hard core. There are also audiences for recorder music for certain kinds of Romantic piano music, for certain sorts of organ music, for certain lieder, for certa varieties of contemporary music, for English music of the late nineteenth and early twentieth centurie for certain types of American music, for Charles Ives, and so on. Each of these forms a small core of t potential sales, often a very small core indeed, and certainly not enough to let the record break even.

We can see from this that the importance of an audience is that it is willing and able to understa the connections of things, whereas a market does not understand connections. The audience will take the benefit of an experience with the work of a previously unknown artist or composer and extrapolat it to an interest in whatever else that artist or composer might do. It will keep itself informed. It will, therefore, directly affect which records are made and by whom. Producers who make records for the operatic audience (and who are frequently members of that audience themselves) do so with the idea that they will be leading the audience somewhere. They do not expect to sell an obscure opera blindly to a market unfamiliar even with relatively well-known operas. They hope to do some of that, of cour but they are banking on the audience at least to pay the costs of the record. They therefore either con sciously, or perhaps unconsciously, using their own tastes and interests as a barometer, make records that they think will interest an audience. This is not the view of the company that issues another set of Beethoven's nine symphonies.

What we derive from this is that the audience *can* be important. If the record producer knows that an audience is there, he will make a great many records that should be made and skip over making a great many that shouldn't or needn't be. After all, it is largely the ego of the performing musician that makes him want to record all the repertoire for his instrument, despite the insane multiplication of performances that will result, but it is the potential for profit that makes the record company go along with him. For, since every record on the market is product, every record is a one-shot. The odd on every one-shot are not the same, just as the odds on every horse in a race are not the same, but it is horse race nevertheless, and any one can win. With an audience to play to rather than a market, the horse race largely disappears. Connections from one event to the next are established, and people have sufficient sophistication to make up their own minds about things and to follow a course of listening for their own pleasure that has some logic to it.

This being so, one wonders why no one has ever tried to *establish* an audience for classical music on records. Records are, due to the imagination of producers and performing artists, the major field today in which experiments are made, reputations built. The success of the symphonies of Gustav Mahler in the concert hall is a direct outgrowth of interest in the recordings of those symphonies. The works of Carl Nielsen, similarly. The works of Charles Ives, certainly. Vladimir Horowitz re-established his reputation through recordings; Vladimir Ashkenazy first established his the same way. One might point to hundreds of artists and at least dozens of composers—to say nothing of the incredible expansion of the known Baroque repertoires—that have become familiar the same way.

But record companies, which will do anything (within financial reason) to build a market, have rather scrupulously avoided doing anything to build an audience. How does one build an audience? By making music so familiar to people at such an early age that they accept it as a normal part of life and, to varying degrees, pursue it themselves. Record companies could, for example, make sure that every elementary-school class had a record player and records to go with it—not sell them at a profit, but give them away or sell them at no profit at all—to build the beginnings of a future audience. But they don't do that, for that is long-range planning, and record companies, like almost all businesses today, are interested in the short run.

Money is not the only reason. A non-profit record company was begun recently by a foundation. I was briefly called in as a consultant. The expressed purpose of the company was to create a series of one hundred records of American music, in honor of the U.S. Bicentennial, the material to be leased or recorded fresh, depending upon availability. I wanted to know what the audience was for this collection of records. It was to be given away, I was told, to certain libraries, music schools, and other institutions, and made available at cost to other institutions. I asked if more good could not be accomplished by making a set of *ten* records and giving it away, together with an inexpensive record player, to, say, every elementary school in the state of Georgia. They looked at me as if I were crazy, and I ceased to be a consultant.

Yet I continue to believe that the formation of an audience for classical music in the United States is a worthy objective. Schools obviously don't believe it. The few students who independently develop a real interest in classical music are immediately thought to be freaks of a sort and, as freaks, are encouraged to become *professional* musicians. We have today perhaps too many professional musicians, too many composers. It would have been far better had many of them been encouraged to be an audience, and let the professional performers and composers come out from that audience on the basis of an undeniable calling. But among students in my generation, and I dare say in most generations that have followed it, just liking classical music was freakish. If you liked it, you had to make it, and if you made it, you had to do it professionally. This produces for everyone what could euphemistically be called an audience of one's peers. If we drop the euphemism, it means a closed society for the protection of each other's egos. So even the musicians seem to have a vested interest in not establishing a real audience; that might produce a group of people who made demands, who said, "Hey, you're supposed to be making music, and making records, for *me.*" And apparently no one—not the record companies, not the librarians, not the musicologists, not the musicians, not the composers, not the critics, not the educators—wants that. It's a pity.

CHRISTOPHER CAMPBELL: You talk about making records widely available to kids in elementary schools, to gradually build up an audience for classical music. On the other hand, you say that today, among, say, my generation, the wide availability of recorded music and the fact that we listen to so much of it make us jaded and insensitive to it. I wonder if that's not rather contradictory.

JAMES GOODFRIEND: We're talking about two different ages. I'm talking about something like first or second or third grade, and I think you're talking about high school and college. I think that if children in the lower grades of elementary schools were exposed to classical music to the extent that it became a natural part of their lives; if every class in the schools had a phonograph and records; if the schools, with the cooperation of record companies, would make available at cost a phonograph and records to every child in the class who wanted to buy them—if all of this happened, then the kids would have some basis on which to make their own further explorations and could, I think, develop into a genuine audience.

CHARLES HAMM: Two points: I don't really understand why children should be subjected to classical music as opposed to jazz, Indian sitar music, or any other type of music. Second, your suggestio if carried out, implies a captive audience. I wonder how you disassociate that from Muzak, if you do.

GOODFRIEND: Well, let me answer it backwards. I make the disassociation very simply, on the basi of the greater good. One has to decide in advance that an audience for classical music is a valuable thing to have. If one decides that, the rest follows. If you disagree with that, then obviously there are problems.

On your first point: Yes, I am talking basically about classical music, mostly, I think, because it doesn't support itself. As far as the record companies are concerned, their most marginal product is classical music. Jazz manages to support itself; these days, I think, it's really quite successful commercially. Pop music, obviously, has no need of special support: the kids get pop music surrounding them the minute they leave school. The thing is to try to equalize matters by giving them some experience of other things. As far as Indian sitar music goes—well, it's not a normal part of Western culture, but I'm certainly not against it.

AUDIENCE MEMBER: What do you think accounts for the lowered interest in classical music today among teenagers compared to when I was a teenager, say thirty-five years ago?

GOODFRIEND: I think it is the overexposure of teenagers to another kind of music and their underexposure to classical music. I hear many times from people in the broadcasting industry that the best composers these days are those who write singing commercials—that this obviously must be so, becaus everybody goes around singing the commercials in their heads. But, of course, what they never take into account is that if you took Webern's *Five Movements for String Quartet* and programmed it on the radio with the frequency with which the Schaefer beer commercial is programmed you might have people walking around singing themes from Webern, too. Rote and repetition produce familiarity, an familiarity produces liking.

JOSHUA RIFKIN: Is it not possible, though, that if we heard Webern's *Five Movements* day in and day out on our AM radios it would turn us into passive, drone-like accepters of Webern and not appreciative audiences of him?

III

THE PHONOGRAPH AND THE COMPOSER

The session of THE PHONOGRAPH AND OUR MUSICAL LIFE that was concerned with the effect on the contemporary composer of the phonograph and sound recording had four composers as panelists—Charles Dodge, William Bolcom, Roger Reynolds, and Eric Salzman. All of them are represented on commercial recordings, and all of them, to varying degrees, have composed "tape music"—that is, have included pre-recorded material as a part of, or the whole of, their compositions. American-music historian H. Wiley Hitchcock chaired the session. (Mr. Dodge's paper, which relied heavily on tape-recorded sound, is not reproduced here.)

William Bolcom

COMPOSER, PERFORMER, AND RECORDINGS

I grew up in very small towns around Seattle, in the years before the second World War. It was not so easy to find or hear a lot of music. When Mr. Petrillo's American Federation of Musicians struck the record industry in 1942, I wrote a letter in my five-year-old hand to him saying, "I wish you the very worst of luck, Mr. Petrillo, because you have made it impossible for kids like me to get to know anything about music, because you're not going to let us buy any more recordings." I was very angry at him, because records were really about the only way I could hear a lot of music. The radio simply wasn't broadcasting much, that far from the centers of the world. I did learn a lot of things in libraries, but a large part of my musical information and the most soul-racking musical experiences I had as a kid came from some very important recordings. One was Stravinsky's *Rite of Spring* on 78 r.p.m.'s—not the 1956 one conducted by Stravinsky but the one that came before it—in 1943, I think. This absolutely changed my life. I played it over and over again. The whole house was going crazy—my parents, my sister, and my grandmother kept begging me to take it off—but I was absolutely fascinated by it, and it changed my life as a musician and as a composer. My next most important landmark was the 78-r.p.m. recording of John Kirkpatrick playing the "*Concord*" *Sonata* of Charles Ives. That also had a terrific influence on me.

As I think back on those now, what struck me most was a combination of two things: the importance of the pieces and the incandescence and conviction of the performances. Both of them, although they were recorded, were obviously based in the performers' minds on a live-music conception of the pieces. I would guess that Kirkpatrick's years of knowing Ives, working with him, steeping himself in that particular work, were the things that made that recording and the music speak to me as strongly as it did. I've heard subsequent recordings by much better-fingered people, and I've certainly heard better performances of *The Rite of Spring* by people who were far more able conductors than Stravinsky, but I've never felt that sense of immediate communication.

So I come to a basic question: is a recording a record of a piece or of a performance? I think that what we have done is to confuse these things. For example, when a work of mine has been recorded, there is a tendency for people to take that performance as an authoritative reading of the piece. A perfectly decent person comes up to me and says, "We have been playing the recording by Bill Albright of your *Black Host,* and have been trying to get our organist to do exactly what Mr. Albright does. We feel that this is a definitive recording. Do you think that's right?" I say, "Well, I think it's a wonderful recording. I'm terribly happy with what Bill did with the piece: I really wrote it with him in mind, and I knew very well the kind of player he is, and obviously all of that fed into the performance on that record. But I would be equally delighted to find some other person taking the same notes and, in their own way, reading into the piece their own particular kind of excitement." Joan Morris and I work a lot with early recordings of the pieces we do. But it's out of the question for us just to imitate those early performances. For one thing, our sense of tempo—our internal, physical tempo—is different from the tempo-sense of 1902, or 1908, or even 1973. Joan Morris's performance of, say, May Irwin's "Frog Song" is a lot *like* May Irwin's version, but it still is essentially different: both performers have got through the *performance* to the *piece.* If Joan had, on the other hand, taken the performance by May Irwin as her basic text, you would get no real sense of either Joan Morris or the piece; you would have only an imitation of a performance.

Now, the reason I mention all of this is that I have a very nasty suspicion that a lot of performers today who hear recorded performances are stuck on that first level of performance. We have more and more people picking as basic texts for their performances recordings they have bought. This has tended, I think, to regularize performers to the extent that now you can turn on an FM radio station and find that part of a Beethoven sonata has been very neatly spliced into another person's performance of the sonata, without any great shock as far as style is concerned. I also think that a kind of scientific attitude on behalf of super-perfection has begun to creep into performances, perhaps due to recording possibilities. This may actually, in fact, go back to Mr. Edison himself. People who knew him have said he did have a kind of optimum-performance ideal, perhaps because he was a nineteenth-century scientist who shared the nineteenth century's aims for perfection. He did not like to record some of the most famous performers, because they had certain faults in vocal production that bothered him. And everyone who recorded for Edison was required to make three complete masters. Anyway, nowadays you have the feeling that performers are in some sort of impossible, quixotic, John-Henry-versus-the-piledriver competition with an edited tape by somebody. And I think this has had an inhibiting effect on performance.

I've always been interested in the theatrical aspect of music. I'm fascinated by the physical presence of the player onstage, and the particular thing that happens when that player gets involved with a piece. That fascinates me. Sometimes I've found that this gets lost in a recording. I wish there were a way to alter the recording situation so that the performer was suddenly inspired to that same kind of application to a piece. One of the things that I would love to see brought back is recording before an audience. I think something would happen—in my own performance, let's say—that doesn't happen when I'm sitting in a freezing church with a location mike miles away, I can't see anyone, and I'm performing to that fourth chandelier over there by the balcony, hoping maybe I can make it rustle a little I need more than that kind of feedback. I'm very old-fashioned in that. I can't do it for *nobody,* nor can I compose for *nobody.* It's much easier for me to write as a composer for some living presence—somebody I know—and I think that may possibly be true of other people. I wonder if this simple solution might reverse the kind of impersonality that seems to have developed, I think, to a great extent in performances on recordings—and also, by extension, off recordings.

WILEY HITCHCOCK: I'm struck by the fact that here we have a composer who indeed spoke as a composer and insisted on his being one, and yet was concerned so much with performance. As Bill Bolcom spoke, I realized that all four of the composers at this table are, in fact, vitally concerned with performance matters: Roger Reynolds with his pieces; Eric Salzman, known particularly for his music-theater pieces, which he directs like an impresario; Charles Dodge with his latest emphases on performer, composer, technician, record producer, and everything.

ERIC SALZMAN: Well, it is true that for a decade already the act of composing music has not been enough, and that the activities of both creating music and getting it performed have tended to merge. This is not a surprise. It's always been true historically, and it's true in most cultures. The activities of composition and performance got separated largely in the nineteenth century, in a society that became increasingly specialist-oriented, but, for a whole lot of reasons, those functions have tended to come back together again. For one thing, the existing institutions, which were created for Classical and Romantic music, are not responsive to contemporary concerts; that alone is enough of a reason to go out and make your own institutions or create your own performance situations.

The place where this might connect with our theme of recorded music is that in response to the possibility of tape music—by which I mean the kind of music that's not meant to be performed by live performers but to be played through speakers—there was a tremendous reaction by people in all sorts of areas, and a rethinking about the activity of live performance. So we got the new improvisation, aleatory, music theater, all kinds of ways in which live performance was reconsidered. I think it's a very characteristic and a very contemporary concern.

HITCHCOCK: Do you share that view, Roger?

ROGER REYNOLDS: Yes, we clearly do not live in a time when the cultural apparatus is naturally amenable to current products. And what that means is that any composer who cares about having his music performed must take on himself some of the responsibility for *getting* it performed.

JOSHUA RIFKIN: It troubles me a little to see the poor phonograph, the hand that is currently feeding us (and we all apparently have some need to be biting), be somehow made responsible for all of the things that we find not to our liking in performance today. I fail, quite honestly, to see the connection.

WILLIAM BOLCOM: Well, then maybe you've never had that trouble, but I think a lot of performers have. They haven't separated in their own mind the piece and the performance. If you can do that readily, you're one of the lucky ones.

RIFKIN: I think that performers always had that trouble, long before the phonograph. The phonograph may have accentuated the difficulty, but I don't think it created it.

BOLCOM: I didn't say it did. But a recording has authority. It has the same authority as the printed word versus the written one. When we see something in print, there is a natural tendency to believe it simply because it's been printed. It's got to be true: it's been printed; somebody's bothered. It's related to the theory that if you're going to fire somebody you should fire him over the telephone; don' fire him face to face. Over the phone there's an impersonality which makes it absolutely final. There something of that impersonal authority in a performance on a recording.

Roger Reynolds

THOUGHTS ON WHAT A RECORD RECORDS

The proliferation of formats by means of which recorded sound can now reach us obliges us to recognize the existence of an image more fundamental than a disc of various diameters, more basic than the many rounded packages within which we now find information lying spiraled. It has led me to a consideration, first, of *storage*: the process of collection and retention. Storage, in turn, implies *access*. Although these two images are computer-related, the following remarks by no means attempt an information-processing approach. Indeed, the phonographic theme—that is, the storage, the reproduction, and the dissemination of *records* in the most general sense—is so vast in its implications that any effort at comprehensiveness is out of place here. My attempt will be to probe towards some of the phenomenon's roots, and to sound a note of caution rather than the admiration and gratitude for the medium that come easily to mind. It is a caution that arose intuitively and deepened as I grappled with notions that clustered under four headings: *storage, subject matter, perspective,* and *dissemination and use.*

Storage

Storage is at first thought a welcomed privilege. It suggests prudence and foresight. But as the variety of techniques by means of which we can store increases, and if little attention is paid to the amount of space that will be required to store, in turn, that which has been stored, economics in one guise or another forces action. Such a process led, for example, to the economies of the LP as compared to 78-r.p.m. records; more recently, to the further space-savings of mini-cassettes and, indeed, to the digital storage of sonic information. These "solutions" are evasive, however, in that they misguide our concern, deflecting it from focusing directly on the phenomenon of storage itself to focusing on short-term relief of its problems.

Another type of storage of greater antiquity, the written word and its various host media (books letters, broadsides), is more neutral by far than the electronic and mechanical conventions that now allow us to save traces of actual events. Words evoke or provoke, but they remain references with wid tolerances when used to inscribe records of actual events. The variety of implications which a spoken phrase can be given by a shift of intonation or the inclination of an eyebrow underscores the relative neutrality of printed messages as compared to more direct sensory experience.

If a medium is not neutral, we may infer that its effect upon us involves at least two domains. One might use "substance" to refer to the selection and the control of interaction between elements of the materials themselves. But the vividness, the palpable extension, of a momentarily arresting event into a continuing engagement with the media's presentation, can also dominate our awareness, especially in the case of short-lived or novel transmissions. I will call this "eventness." The comments below under "Subject Matter" discuss this dual aspect of the phonograph and its progeny, which represent a far from neutral medium.

There are other constraints inherent in the scope of any recording process, some as obvious as length, if one wishes to conserve the continuities of originals not designed for commercially motivated packages (although in the days of 78s the musically arbitrary partitioning of revered continuities was accepted, almost without a grumble). A more significant limit is that of contexts. These include *temporal contexts* (the state of the art, technology, recording contracts, international relationships, and musicological scholarship, for example, at the time a series of recording sessions is scheduled); *physical context* (the recording space chosen and its relationship to the size and spatial disposition of sonorous sources within it, the temperature and humidity of the air, not to mention the untoward incursion of creaks, coughs, or passing trains); or, more subtly, a composite of *psychological factors* (the relationships—the human resonances potential and struck—between performers, materials, and space on a particular day). Striking more deeply into these contexts, one might consider both the number of sensory modes involved in a record as well as the sophistication with which each is dealt. For instance: a program note, to which is added a sonic trace, to which is added a visual record. But is the sonic record monaural, stereophonic, or quadraphonic? What of the signal-to-noise ratio? The dynamic range? The spatial definition? And so on.

Whatever attention is devoted to optimizing these various contexts, the resulting record will be decisively colored and tailored, and will continue to represent its origins rigidly. Depending upon our proclivities, upon changing evaluations of the meaning and merit of the original musical event, we may cherish the ability to recheck and, in a sense, revisit a momentary confluence of numerous variables. That is a positive side of the unchanging record. A negative aspect is that recording may arbitrarily elevate the meaning and influence of what is, after all, only one particular train of moments—each an evanescent, unreproducible outcome of interactive processes. I am not quite wrong-headed enough to assert that moments—and especially those of a more special cast—should be left alone and allowed to pass irrevocably, but I would enjoy hearing such a position argued.

There is fundamental ambiguity in the public consciousness regarding the unique quality of experience as directly lived, on the one hand, and packaged experiences as editorially contrived, on the other. The simultaneous development in the marketplace of two opposing approaches confirms it. Digital recording methods only now coming into use promise freedom from noise and other systemic distortions, while offering an editorial capacity that is scarcely to be imagined. Not only may one transfer from one continuity to another seamlessly and remove undesired intrusions; one may elongate and reshape a desirable sound that was perhaps too brief or interrupted in the recording. Complementary developments focus on the direct-to-disc process. One pays handsomely—strangely—for the privilege of hearing the Cleveland Orchestra play an uninterrupted movement as they might actually perform it in concert. Still, we counter only one of the many distortions in the stored reality when we demand that the continuity of the original—flawed or not—be retained.

In the early days of recording, restrictions on the length of the commercial package involved frequent and almost inevitable disruption of original continuities. Tempos were adjusted, repeats deleted, sections excised. Demands made by the medium resulted in evident artistic compromise in interpretive, stylistic, and structural matters. Although the tyranny of package-length is far less pervasive since the advent of long-playing records and, more recently, cassettes, it would be absurd to imagine that intrusions of the storage medium's characteristics into the artist's domain have ceased. Incursions are inevitable, and we should, at the very least, be attempting to retain some perspective on the whole: on the distinctions between *original* and *record.* For, to a significant degree, the record is becoming the more available and compelling reference.

Subject Matter

A decisive early stimulant to my musical curiosity was a recording of the Chopin A-flat Polonai as performed by Vladimir Horowitz. Within a few weeks the original recording had been ground dow to an unintelligible rasp, and a second copy purchased. My fascination was not a result of the underlying pattern of pitch progressions and rhythmic relationships, for I had heard the same work in scho on numerous occasions. A record of this work played by José Iturbi had not similarly galvanized me. What cut so swiftly into my consciousness was the recorded image of the sonority itself, the scope of the dynamic interplay, the relentless tensility that Horowitz brought to his realization of a series of indications that, on paper, holds only potential.

Clearly, there is something of a personal chemistry at work in the powerful and selective response that a listener may have to one or another performer or composer. A variety of performer-listener pairing might well have produced a parallel and comparable stimulus to that which I describec What is significant is the notion that the "subject matter" to which one responds may not be identica with the structure of relationships that identifies the composition, whether sonata or symphony. Rat it may derive from the particular realization: the articulative elaboration, the sensory radiance.

During thought about the storage process, a number of distinctions between "substance" and "eventness" emerged. The first involves the selection of certain musical forces, the materials they are asked to deal with, and the specification of how these factors will interact. The determination of substance as here outlined might be accomplished through carefully detailed plans or by more general improvisatory guide lines. The substance of recordings comes, then, from a more or less extended train decision-making. In the more traditional situation, a creative person conceives the musical work as a notated product or an improvisatory expression of ingrained structural and stylistic values. This work is then stored in a performance that is the final stage in the representation of its substance.

More recently, recording has provided the possibility of an additional stage in the process. It ha done so by allowing the compilation and superimposition of materials that are already fully formed a self-contained. This is a higher-order operation in an architectural sense, and its harbinger has been th often decisive importance of the producer for rock-group recordings. Assembling arrays of extravagar diverse materials on multiple-track tapes, the producer then mixes and/or rearranges elements that are to say the least, improbable as the coordinated products of a single composer (for the composer's concerns have generally been more focused or elemental).

Substance comes to us through performance realizations. These only occasionally take on the extraordinary qualities of definition and fancy that raise the presentation to a vividness that overrides its component events. The smaller segments from which this curious "eventness" arises might be term "moments." By this is meant particularly dynamic or subtle realizations of the details of any work's substance. Sometimes such "moments" are caught by chance through the routine recording of a performance not primarily intended as an occasion for storage. As with "substance," the medium—the process of storage itself—has added another dimension to the discovery and incorporation into documents of moments of distinction. Now an eventness of sorts—an unlikely string of singular moments—can be *fabricated* by an extended process of collection, assessment, and editing. The listener is led int accepting—indeed, relishing—a chain of events that are perfectly executed and variously enhanced in sonic substance. Each component moment may itself have been a product of some accidental enlargement through fortuitous but unpredictable circumstances. Such moments can be snatched from more mundane surroundings and incorporated into a newly constructed continuity.

The skills of both the editor and the producer are directed towards the unreal, even the supra-real, representation through recording of musical performance; but they have gone far beyond whatever minimal levels of neutrality the medium might be said to possess. They are able to create a previously unimagined class of replicated "occasions for experience"—to use Peter Yates's phrase—that have no analog in real life. It is characteristic of recording as an industry to have given us access not only to what *is* but also to what *could never be* . . . well, almost never. As the distinctions blur, it is useful to pause and try to identify, from time to time, the subject matter to which we are *actually* responding.

Perspective

No foreseeable technology could enable us to actually revisit (let alone relive) the precise circumstances attending any musical performance. These circumstances include not only the physical facts, the patterns of pressure differences in the air; just as fundamental are the necessarily unique memories and capacities of each observer, as well as the way in which he or she distributes attention during the performance. We are incessantly changed. We thus grow—even if forgetful—unendingly new in our expectations and responses. Since objective and holistic preservation is beyond reach, we might quite reasonably inquire into the biases that our personal perspectives entail. Each act of storage involves a standpoint taken, a perspective assumed.

The recording industry includes persons of diverse persuasions about what constitutes a "natural" or an "ideal" recorded sound. An anecdote about an experience that instructed me a few years ago: I had written a work for chamber ensemble and, utilizing spatially separated instrumental groups, incorporated patterns of spatially defined "motives" into the composition. This fact was clearly spelled out in the printed score's introductory notes. Appearing, by chance, at the final editing sessions for a stereo recording destined for commercial release, I was perplexed to note a sense of dimension which included depth and resonance but lacked left-right differentiation. I was informed that the motival structure that was intrinsic to the work's architecture had been, in effect, suppressed, because the recording engineer disliked the "ping-pong effect."

This recollection of mine is meant only to suggest that engineers and producers of quality have carefully nurtured concepts of perspective, metaphoric positions that they feel are "natural" or, if not that, "ideal" in some sense. Of course *all* acts of storage involve perspective, whether by chance or design, and I am drawing attention to those that are, so to speak, premeditated and thus perhaps open to discussion.

The use of microphones, our "extended ears," is crucial. Human beings have, inescapably, a bilateral symmetry, and will in the end reduce any multiplicity of audio input into chains of pulses travelling up the two auditory nerves. Temporally, the finest discriminations of which human beings are capable occur in assessing the differences between similar signals arriving almost simultaneously at the two ears. Although this pair of receptors is separated by only half a foot, it allows us to make discriminations on the order of one hundred-thousandth of a second. My point is that, however many ersatz probes we extend into our aural surroundings, the end product will allow, at most, two streams of information to undergo scrutiny within us. The use of four-track, eight-track, sixteen-track tape recorders (and some have even more) emphasizes the prerogatives of the person responsible for mixing down such an input (perhaps suited to a myriad-eared Deva) to its eventual bi-lateral form. But any time more than two microphones are used, a mixing decision, and therefore a perspectival distortion, is introduced at some level. This is not a brief for conservativism in recording technique nor a broadside at the industry. In fact, the enhanced and warped audio spaces into which we can be placed, by multiple microphones tactically arrayed, is one of the new and useful resources for which we can be grateful, in principle. What concerns me are the long-term effects of the continuous and variegated manipulation of aural perspective in recordings. By "perspective" I mean in part the physical position in which one might imagine oneself while hearing a particular record. Close your eyes and try listening to an orchestral recording that includes both tutti and soloistic elements. Try to get your physical bearings. Balances are produced, relative intensities and proximity cues are manipulated, in a way that is quite unimaginable in any real performance situation.

As a composer, I have in the past few years recorded sounds as material to be incorporated into tapes that will accompany performance on live instruments. It can be a vexing task. The experience has led me to the edge of what is surely a vast chasm of as yet distant and dimly perceived possibilities for supra-real perspectives. If we knew what we were doing—or, more to the point, what was being done to us—if there were some systematic exploration of perspective, we could confidently anticipate the emergence of a positive new resource. As it is, one has to wonder at the various, the unreal, the inconsistent images with which we are constantly in contact. By their rigidity, omnipresence, and insistence, they thrust upon us models which cannot be matched in daily experience with live musicians. Some composers and engineers have been trying to explore the ramifications of perspective as I have sketchily outlined them here. My own set of quadraphonic tape works, VOICESPACE, is one such instance. Working on them was a humbling experience. One can hardly resist reference to the "dimensions" of the task. . . .

Dissemination and Use

Once the record exists in some form, we can consider who has access to it and under what conditions. The fact of dissemination has been implicit in much of the preceding. Its very scope is, of course, significant; but a wide-reaching impact may be generated by touching even a small public if that public's influence has weight. Without proposing an answer, I pose the following question: Is the self-consciousness engendered in musicians (or for that matter in athletes) by the recording and analysis of their performance through repeated playbacks desirable in the long run? An answer would involve assessing the role of technique as contrasted with the strategy of aesthetic or competitive aims. The instructor or commentator is well served by such records, but is the performer?

Another aspect of the "self" and the "other" deserves mention. Recordings allow phenomena that have traditionally been public, or at least minimally communal, to become intimate, even individual, matters. The relationship between the listener and the invariant, hence unresponsive, event (however mirrored by storage) becomes private. The participants in a traditional partnership are now disengaged. Furthermore, listening occurs in what is often a musically irrelevant and unchanging environment. Whether playing back a solo *shakuhachi* performance or the Berlioz *Requiem,* our home listening context remains the same. Of course, the recorded perspective mitigates this by providing auditory cues that point towards an appropriate physical environment. Still, a host of other cues—

visual, tactile, social—attend us always, contriving to skew in one way or another how and what we experience.

As a brief and rather arbitrary exercise, I took from a library nine recordings of the Tchaikovsky B-flat minor Piano Concerto. They included—not at all by design—recordings made in the United States, Europe, and Russia over a period of several decades. Capitalizing on the rhetorical nature of this work's opening, I spliced the first five chords of each recording in series to obtain an insistent cycle that was only allowed to progress after all nine versions had made their appearance. Subsequently, each successive chord was extracted from a different recording until the entrance of the lyric theme in the strings. I did not wish to draw attention to the differences among the recordings with regard to intonation, tempo, orchestral weighting, or acoustical quality but rather to the way in which each cut abruptly shifted the listener's position—our perspective, relative to *them.* Furthermore, how differently "they"—the brass sections, the strings, the piano soloist—were re-situated relative to each other in the different recordings. It is one thing to simulate this inherently large-space experience in a spacious hall in the presence of a large audience, and another to do it solitarily in one's apartment living room. Is this intensification of contrast between the private experience of recordings and the public experience of performance unimportant? How are we to retain the ability to "hear between the grooves" in the face of increasing dissemination of recorded materials and of the proliferating equipment that allows ever greater clarity and intensity of sound reproduction? Intuitively, one feels that any practice which results in elevating the image of the unreal at the expense of the real should be resisted.

Recordings, as mass-produced and distributed, reflect a commercial process. Market-building and exploitation are far more likely imperatives in it than cultural service. We have experienced and can expect continuing efforts on the part of industry to intensify the impact of their products through widened dynamic, timbric, and spatial contrasts, in both the preparation and playback stages of production. There seems little reason to anticipate that commercial labels will lessen their relentless exploration of the basic, familiar repertoire. But their economic bias finds its counterparts in the egalitarian practices of labels dedicated to the interests of large and haphazardly formed composers' societies or the pressures brought to bear by musicological circles in support of exhaustive exhumation. Such an irrepressible surfeit of recordings is not just an illusory potentiality; it is an accomplished and daily compounded fact. Records are *objects* to be bought, collected, imitated, enjoyed. They are not one-of-a-kind, nor do they provide us with the urgency of transient live performance, within the context of which both large outline and moment-to-moment detail pass across our ears irretrievably. To the dangers of rigidity, then, one may add those of multiple copies and indiscriminate repertoire selection.

The ramifications of the capacity and the drive to store are, however, far wider than I have so far suggested. The re-recording of standard repertoire does, of course, allow one to find and evaluate, as might be done through extensive concert-going, the substance of the works themselves. With contemporary compositions, however, the likelihood is that no more than a single recording of any piece will emerge. The singular representation—the existence as sound (though inflexible)—has a tendency to *become* the work, even for the composer. The authority of sound prevails over the abstract prescription in score. The goal (let alone the fact) of multiple realizations fades, and the creative person's aims are inevitably re-directed.

It goes without saying, but should be said often, that the unparalleled number of models available for emulation, the recording artist's editorially achieved infallibility, and the influence upon repertoire that commercially motivated recordings impose on performers have contributed to the shaping of an astonishingly capable but sometimes vaguely homogeneous cadre of younger performers. Composers suffer even more harmful pressures of identity, I believe. They deal, necessarily, with a substance less proven and resilient than the performer's standard repertoire. For the composer, the availability—amounting to unavoidability—of multiple and diverse models is sobering enough as an intra-cultural phenomenon; how much more seductive and perilous these influences can be when they pass to us across cultural boundaries.

Having sounded so many warnings and taken such admittedly extreme positions, I must end by conceding, even affirming, that much is to be gained by the continuing existence and perfection of recorded sound. The general point of my remarks has been, as I said, cautionary. It is imperative that the nature of storage be considered broadly and from a more critical perspective. Corrective measures for certain of the conditions I have identified are not beyond reach: for example, the identification and perhaps standardization of "perspective"; the reining in of editorial prerogatives; the sponsorship of more recordings for personal educational purposes combined with a sharply increased level of discrimination applied to the selection of what is actually disseminated; clear differentiation between those recordings made to commemorate actual performances and of those made to represent unfamiliar segments of repertoire acceptably. The recording process could be more "neutral" than it has become, and this in turn might provide a stimulus to use the power of selective and supra-real sound collection in more openly creative contexts. The accelerating growth of the computer's capacity to store and process audio materials digitally will, of course, compound all of the above. A circumspect respor from those assembled here could be of importance. Let us not celebrate and sanctify too easily.

JAMES GOODFRIEND: I think what Roger really needs is the serious-music equivalent of Mort Sahl' "perfect jazz record"—the one where the solos are different every time you play it.

AUDIENCE MEMBER: I wonder if you could explain a little bit more—on a philosophical basis, I gue —why you see the unreal as dangerous and threatening.

ROGER REYNOLDS: If the models that surround you do not correspond with your real-life experience, that will cause disturbance. Now, it's quite another matter if we eventually come to the point of accepting that there are two streams of information reaching us. But what I was arguing is that there's a great deal of *unconsciousness* in our present attitude toward the recorded experience.

AUDIENCE MEMBER: I think the cautionary note is well taken, but I don't wholly agree, from this point of view: I'm one of those who does not identify the visceral impact of a work with the work itself, and so it seems to me that the job of "listening between the grooves" can be a very invigorating task; it can be very provocative to work back to the original. But I think one simply has to *add* that, in a recorded performance, to the work of putting the aesthetic object together in the first place; that is, it's an additional task. So, for me, a supra-real in new recordings is not necessarily a bad thing. I suppose I'm suggesting the reverse of the cautionary note: I think the supra-real can assist the listener, who has his job to do regardless of the quality of the sound that he has to work with.

REYNOLDS: Your last point suggests an educational process—and I don't mean that at a trivial level—which multiple versions of music *do* allow, and I did try to make that point. And I share your view about the visceral impact versus the work itself. The tangible fact of the experience is essential, but the notion that that experience can have only one form is anathema. When I talk about the generality and power of a score I am referring to the notion that a model of music, of a class of musical experiences, exists, and that this is a Western richness which is extraordinary and not a part of many other musical cultures. It's a richness which I treasure, and, in a certain way, of course, it is challenged in profound ways by recording, particularly by singular recordings of works. William Bolcom made a similar remark, to the effect that you have a tendency sometimes, as a composer, to view a recording of a work of yours as the *piece;* you forget that the work is not that recording.

WILLIAM IVEY: It seems to me that the panel has dealt so far primarily with the impact of recordings on traditional composition, that is, composition which has as its product a score or a manuscript of some sort. But there is a kind of composition that is much better integrated with the recording process, one which has, as its results, synthetic sounds, an event rather than a score. I would like you to comment on the electronic or the computer type of composition, which does seem better integrated with recording technology than, perhaps, the kinds of composition you have been focusing on so far.

REYNOLDS: That's really what I meant when I said that the harbinger of this new capacity of recording had been the rock-group producer. I indicated that I felt this multi-tracked and multi-sourced action was only beginning. It's quite clear that synthesized music, musique concrète, all kinds of collage pieces, and so on are clearly arising from that capacity to deal with pre-existent musical items.

CHARLES DODGE: I've been in the position of having compositions appear on a recording before they were performed—pieces which were created in studios or on computers—yet I find that I still do, nonetheless, distinguish between the composition that I have wrought and the tape that I've made of it. Even when I have a hard time going back to create a different "performance" of the piece, I think I have a notion of the composition as something outside of the tape realization. And I think it's more than just wishful thinking that I'd done a better job. I think it's that the relationships, in the things that I do, stand apart, in some way, from the computer programs and from the dials that I twist. I think that when I go back and re-do one of my pieces it is *that* piece again.

AUDIENCE MEMBER: I have a question to address to each of you, and it's in two parts: first, do you feel that recordings of your own music have in any way contributed to your prominence as a composer? And second, having achieved a degree of prominence, does the existence of a recording as a further document, so to speak, of your music make you feel any more self-conscious or responsible in your work?

BOLCOM: Well, one is published by a recording, so to speak, in a way that one is not published even when one's score is reproduced, and it looks good and is a kind of cachet. It's something that is very nice.

REYNOLDS: The most important function of recordings for me is to give me possible new opportunities to compose. They provide a certain visibility.

BOLCOM: Again, cachet, which is a step toward economic security.

REYNOLDS: No, no, not the economic. It's the opportunity to move ahead. Most composers, I think, are most interested in the work they are just about to write, unless they're doing one right now, and then that's the one they're most interested in. So the thrust is always forward, and the recordings that you've made may give you opportunities to make new pieces. What I wish, ideally, is that I could withdraw recordings from circulation, bit by bit.

BOLCOM: With the deletion policy, it will happen automatically, Roger.

AUDIENCE MEMBER: But doesn't the archival possibility interest you?

REYNOLDS: No. I would much rather have the archive be the score, because that provides, or permi a more general class of events. However, I have made some tape pieces, in which case *they* are the piec no score is involved.

ERIC SALZMAN: The one real advantage of records relates to distribution. The thing that is most sig nificant to me is the size of the audience. And there is no question that with recordings we have a mea of communication and distribution to an exceptionally wide and diverse audience, even at the relativel low market level represented by the kind of music made by the people on this panel. It's a fact that th pieces of mine that are recorded are the best-known ones; also that, of the two albums that are out, the one on Nonesuch Records—which is a company of very wide distribution—is the better-known.

DODGE: There's no question but that recordings have been extremely important in my public positio as a composer, since most of my recordings are of my tape music. To me the best way of distributing i on recording. But what that has to do with me as a composer is another question. I feel a little the wa Bill Bolcom does: records take on a life of their own. Some of my records have sold more copies than my mother has friends, and that pleases me very much. At the same time, it's kind of bewildering.

Eric Salzman

TECHNOLOGY AND RECENT DIALECTICAL PROCESSES IN MUSIC

I am going to talk about a perception that I've had, going back now a decade or so, about technology and its impact on our musical culture. What I'm going to say is a beginning of an analysis that could be made in other areas, not just in music, but I'll limit myself to music. I'll start with some basic facts that I think are unassailable. Perhaps they are obvious, but I don't think that they are clearly und stood by a lot of people.

The percentage of musical experience that comes through loudspeakers is enormous. I would say it probably approaches ninety percent or some such figure. Even with the resurgence of live music—an I think we have had such a resurgence—it's very, very large. It has become thus dominant in the period of the long-playing record and the widespread development of relatively inexpensive, decent playback equipment. It has pervaded every area of musical life and musical culture.

I think also that loudspeaker sound has become more or less the unconscious ideal of our times, and that this is as true of the classical listener or performer as it is of the pop listener or performer. With performers, I think this may have generated a whole performance style. There is a lot of reaction nowadays to what we might call the "modern classical" style of performance—a lot of new romanticism in performance, some of which gets on recordings. But there was a modern classical style of performance which I believe may have been generated by recordings. I think that perhaps it was Arturo Toscanini's hearing playbacks of the recordings of his NBC performances that started that—maybe not literally, but that's my metaphor for it. I think he may have had a whole different perception about music when he was at NBC than earlier; that is, he got to be more and more exclusively a performer for radio and recordings. In any case, whatever the source was, the clean, classical style of performance became very, very pervasive.

Another important aspect of our contemporary musical culture, including institutional aspects—the way music is taught, the way music is listened to, the way music is produced, even the phenomena of neo-classicism and of nostalgic revival, for example, in pop music—is based on the fact that we can re-listen to, re-experience, aspects of musical culture that traditionally have disappeared. One of the important things about our technological musical culture is that it constantly layers the past on us—stacks it up, so to speak—and makes it, in some difficult-to-understand sense, part of the present. This is very new and very strange, and it has many implications. It's part of the reason why we're having problems: we don't really have any cultural perspective for understanding what's happened to us, what's been done to us, because it's been done very fast, and it's happened in every dimension simultaneously.

I'm going to deal principally with the effect of technology, as I see it, on the course of contemporary music. The immediate historical impact was very simple: tape music and electronic music. People saw the possibility of a new creative use of technology that would express something real or important about contemporary life, and they jumped into it. It happened quite early; in fact, as soon as tape became available. With this kind of music, it was possible to conceive of the work of music in an entirely different way: rather than a loose, flexible, changeable thing—whether based on a score or on a traditional kind of communication from performer to performer or period to period—it could be cast immediately in finished, final form. When this first came about, composers like Milton Babbitt, for example, emphasized the fact that it enabled them to put the paint right on the canvas and present it to the public without any intermediary who might be unfaithful to a work or betray it in some way.

Then, what is interesting is that a reaction to this set in. I believe in the reality of dialectical processes, and I think that the history of musical culture in the last several decades shows very clearly the operation of dialectical processes. Composers looked at the finished perfection of tape-recorded music and they decided to have another look at the process of music in live performance, and a lot of new ideas came flooding into the field. Composers began to become involved in the variability of live performance as something to start out with as a *premise.* This brought about the development of ideas of chance, of aleatory, of improvisational elements in musical performance. Even though I realize that, to some, John Cage and his group seemed to have *proposed* such ideas, I really see their flowering as a *reaction*—a dialectical reaction to tape-recording as a possible means of achieving a finished, final form. Thus we can almost say that recording technology generated that first phase of post-World War II musical development.

But I see it as having gone still further than that. There was another phase, related to, and as I see it generated by, the increasing amount of information that was becoming available in recorded form. By "information" I mean all sorts of things. I mean multiple musics of world cultures; I mean bird songs; I mean recordings exploring the distant past and lesser-known composers, or composers like Ives who had never been successful in concerts. I mean noise and its incorporation in music—say, in musique concrète or the works of Varèse, but also becoming part of everyday experience on radio and television, film sound-tracks, and so forth. There was, in short, an enormous and sudden widening of auditory experience, so that musical culture, which had formerly proceeded in a certain line and ha been relatively limited in any one time and place, got caught up in this multiplicity of events, in this bombardment. In the sixties we used to hear a lot of talk about information overload and sensory bom bardment, and there was a lot to that.

It seems to me that a new dialectic has arisen out of this auditory bombardment. It was necessar for all of us to deal with it, but especially for creative people and composers to do so—to make a choic between facing up to it or ruling it out, between finding a way to cope with it or pushing it away. In music, these two approaches don't have any definitive names. The term "minimal art," referring to th rejection of multiplicity, is one that was very widely circulated and had specific reference in the visual arts, and I see a parallel to this in the works of certain composers. There's a very great difference between the work of La Monte Young, let's say, and the ideas of Steve Reich or Terry Reilly or Phil Glas But there is a parallel between them in that they have chosen to deal with the multiplicity and comple of experience by ruling most of it out, and to try to understand some very simple basic area of experie by delving into it in depth. This has provided one major stream of contemporary music.

The other stream--I hate to use the word "maximalist" because it's an awful term—has been an a tempt to deal with this multiplicity of aural experience by sublimating it and turning it into some kind work of art, by exploiting that very diversity. There are a lot of examples of this. The most obvious e amples in the 1960s (and now I'm speaking personally, because it was the route that I chose) were the multi-media idea itself, and then any number of works which have been classified under various terms, among them "the new eclecticism."

I'd like to add a few words about my own work, since in fact as a composer I consciously reacte to this matter and dealt with it, particularly in my works of the '60s. My own conclusions today are slightly different than they were in the '60s, but my awareness of this dialectic influenced my work ve directly in the '60s and produced a couple of pieces which, logically enough, found their way into reco ed form. In fact, one work was basically intended and conceived for recording. It's actually my best-known work: *The Nude Paper Sermon,* which was commissioned by Nonesuch Records. I originally had the idea of doing a work which would be realizable in either recorded or live performance. But wh has happened with that work is exactly what was said earlier: the recorded form has become the "live" form of the work. The work, as it has been performed live since the record came out, is nearly always done in that version. It would be difficult to change that at this point, I think; it could be changed, bu right now the recording remains the determinant of the image of the work.

My notion was to produce a piece that was, in effect, a multi-media or, at any rate, a dramatic work in sound—that is, to use various layers and elements of sound experience as its structural premise Since the performing organization was more or less determined by the character of the commission, th had a great deal to do with it. The performing organization was a consort of singers and instrumentalists whose basic though not exclusive premise was early music; this was the Nonesuch Consort, conduct by Joshua Rifkin. So the concept of a Renaissance consort was a very important one, and one of the first things that occurred to me was that Renaissance music was something that we had come to know best through the medium of recordings—we heard it through a kind of window, which was the loudspeaker. The very opening of the work has a kind of a babble of voices, and out of that comes a sound of pseudo-Renaissance music heard in perspective, with lots of echo put in to suggest depth and distance. And, just to make sure that it was clear that you were listening through a window, I put electronic sounds over it (I called them graffiti) which were completely on the surface of the speaker— a madrigal with electronic graffiti. Another premise of the piece was the notion of verbal versus non-verbal sound. The verbal sound was embodied in one of the principal characters of the piece, an actor who is like a narrator.

Here were a lot of things already: language versus music; Renaissance sounds representing tradition; the electronic present. They give an idea of some—even if by no means all—of the premises out of which the piece was built. It was then recorded on multiple tracks, which were individually edited, then montaged with live overlays onto an eight-track master; this was then mixed down to a final two-track master.

Example: Excerpt from beginning of Part Two of *The Nude Paper Sermon* (Nonesuch H-71231).

I'll end on a somewhat personal note. I have thought a great deal about the matter of where technology leaves us, with regard to the actual practice of music, the actual business of playing and singing. I've come to the conclusion that musical culture is basically what people do, not what they hear. The hearing process is an intrinsic part of it and cannot be separated, but that it is *only* a part has been emphasized for us by technology, because technology has given us such a clear and sharp distinction between doing music, or making music, and listening to it. To return to what I said in the earlier discussion: You put out a record, and it becomes your best-known work, and it's heard by far more people than ever hear it in live performance. But you don't know who those people are. You've lost contact with the audience; you don't know what the audience is; in fact, it's probably very difficult to define the audience in any real way. Furthermore, the feedback that you get from that audience is non-existent or very much delayed and hard to understand. It seems as if the traditional institutions that exist don't answer this problem. You can't go back to them and try to revitalize them very much. So we all go out and try to make our own music: we form groups, we do this, we do that. That's healthy; it's good that that's happened. But it seems to me that the problem of the forum musical performance can take place in, where the composer can operate, is still a very, very difficult one. We don't have many institutions to make it possible, and even the best ones we have are not so great. In the '60s we all thought it was a great thing to go into a rock club, you know, like the Electric Circus, and do things there, because at least that was a kind of institution. But what's happened to rock? It's gone back into the concert hall, into an institutionalized forum that's not responsive. And the concert hall has become a pale imitation of the recorded form.

This is the reason why theater has become very meaningful to me. Looking at the history of music, I find that music and theater have a traditional relationship that has been very fruitful. And theater is our last non-technological handicraft cottage industry. Now, of course, when you find out that Transamerica Corporation or Pepsi-Cola or somebody is putting on Broadway shows, mainly with the idea of the record sales, you begin to wonder also about theater. But at least theater continues to flourish to some extent, if sometimes in off-beat ways, and it continues to have a real audience: it co tinues to provide feedback, in a social setting where people get together. Since my own inclinations were already in that direction, I have a strong feeling that some kind of a contemporary music theater is a very, very important object for us. And, as I look at it, I realize that this perspective that I have—of the importance of the live performance, the importance of theater, the importance of social ritual—is partly my way of dealing with this whole phenomenon of technology.

Ten or fifteen years ago, we thought that if we could get hold of the means of the technology we could humanize it; we could fight fire with fire. That no longer seems so true today; it seems more and more difficult. Therefore, we see the creation of alternate institutions of one kind or another as means for communication—institutions that perhaps escape, to some degree, the overpowering influence of technology.

RICHARD CRAWFORD: Mr. Salzman's remarks prompt me to ask a question I've had in mind for some time, particularly because I think it has quite a bit to do with the phonograph. I'm struck, in what you say, by your sense of being, on the one hand, a composer and, on the other, someone with a very clearly articulated view of history, and thus, obviously, a view of your own place in it. One of th difficult things about composing nowadays must be confronting this very fact. Something Roger Reynolds said relates to this too—that is, the inescapability of all these influences, and all this music, that seems to be around. Do you have a view of yourself as somehow trying to resolve historical issue as well as being somebody who sits down and creates a piece of music? And is that burden or advanta

ERIC SALZMAN: If you have been brought up and trained in the classical music tradition in this cou try, you are burdened with history; it's been laid on you from a very early age.

CRAWFORD: Your view of history as well?

SALZMAN: Well, whether it's a conscious view of history or not, you have to deal with it. The day when even a jazz musician or a popular musician is a so-called "noble-savage" who just emotes is past, by and large. Even they have some view of history, whether it's an intellectual, Marxist, or whatever kind of view.

ROGER REYNOLDS: For me the understanding of where we've been, or the articulation of where w think we have been, is totally different from trying to articulate where we are not. And, as a compose if I were to understand fully the problem with which I am grappling in a work, I would discard it as an effort, because the only meaning of the effort lies in the attempt to deal with issues which are not cle graspable. Compositionally, I am only interested in those things that have that attractive vagueness th will pull me into a full-scale involvement with a piece.

SALZMAN: My interest in history is only really in its meaning as of the moment. I agree with Roger Reynolds, although we might not reach the same conclusions: the past means something only in term of this historical moment, this moment of me as a person—who is the result, of course, of history. Th thing is that technology has made this more crucial, because it constantly brings up the past in waves against us; it makes it more palpable.

AUDIENCE MEMBER: A positive note toward the future: there exists now a video-disc player that can play something like hundreds of hours of music, and, of course, video tape, so that Bill Bolcom can bring back the live-performance component, and maybe the composer won't be hindered any more.

WILLIAM BOLCOM: I have a question about all of this: Why this incredible need to preserve and record? Why such a terrific driving urge to do this?

SAM PARKINS: How come we have so many books, Bill?

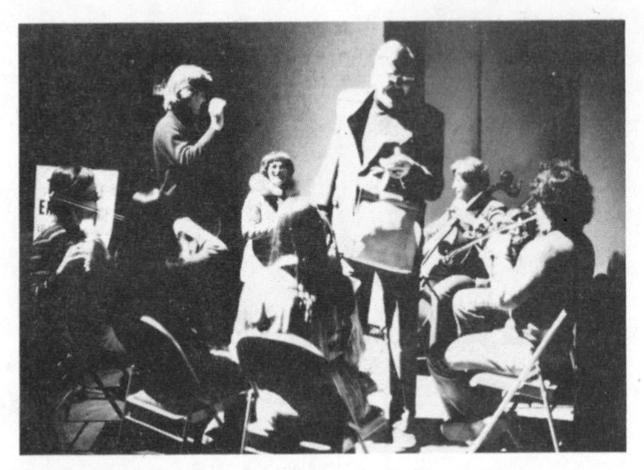

Walking through Erik Satie's *Musique d'ameublement*, on the way to John Cage's *Address*.

Moments before the "Response" to John Cage's *Address.*

Performers of the premiere of John Cage's *Cassette*. From left: Richard Crawford, Vivian Perlis, Charles Hamm, Stoddard Lincoln, and H. Wiley Hitchcock.

Participants in the session on "The Composer and the Audience."
From left: James Goodfriend, William Ivey and Joshua Rifkin.

Composers Roger Reynolds, left, and William Bolcom.

Composer Eric Salzman and, behind him, H. Wiley Hitchcock.

Rock historian and record producer Charlie Gillett.

Jane Jarvis, left, and Joan Peyser (editor of *The Musical Quarterly*).

Musicologist Richard Crawford.

Cynthia Adams Hoover and, behind her, Claire Brook.

Participants in the session on "The Scholar and Critic."
From left: John Rockwell, William Malm, and David Hamilton.

Conference directors Rita H. Mead and H. Wiley Hitchcock.

Photographs by Suzanne Mead.

IV

THE PHONOGRAPH AND THE PERFORMER

All four of the panelists in the session of THE PHONOGRAPH AND OUR MUSICAL LIFE dealing with the impact on performers of recording technology have been involved with recording projects. Martin Williams and David Baker are both associated with the jazz world. Charlie Gillett is a historian of rock-and-roll, and also a record producer. William Ferris is a folklorist who has recorded many Mississippi Delta bluesmen. Chairing the session was Stoddard Lincoln, a harpsichordist and critic of classical-music recordings. (Mr. Ferris's paper, "Records as seen by Mississippi Delta Bluesmen," has been published as a chapter in his book Blues from the Delta *[Garden City: Anchor Press/Doubleday, 1978], pp. 51-54, and is not reproduced here.)*

Martin Williams

JAZZ, THE PHONOGRAPH, AND SCHOLARSHIP

My tasks in the Smithsonian Institution's Division of Performing Arts are primarily neither schol arly nor curatorial. The Division is there as a part of the Smithsonian's efforts to be, in the phrase of the Secretary, S. Dillon Ripley, a "museum without walls," and we put performers on stages to do wh ever they do before audiences. As Director of the Jazz Program, I produce monthly concerts during th theatrical season. The program leaflets for these concerts carry, in part, the following words:

> It has been said that jazz and its remarkable history have been intrinsically tied to the pho graph record. Through recordings, the musical word spread rapidly, a creative player's inn vations could be absorbed quickly. A trumpeter in St. Louis, or an orchestrator in New Y could learn of (and if capable, build on) the contributions of a player from New Orleans al most overnight. At the same time, jazz is a player's art, and however much we might learn from the musical notation of a brilliant improvisation by Charlie Parker, or from studying the score of an Ellington work, we learn vastly more by hearing them played by Parker, or the Ellington orchestra. And if we can no longer hear Parker or Ellington, we can hear their records. . . .

The pioneer writers on jazz in the 1930s recognized that improvisational jazz was uniquely suite to the phonograph, which could preserve for posterity—in an ultimate twentieth-century American pa dox—music which was sometimes made up on the spur of the moment, and which has repeatedly dem strated, I am convinced, that an impromptu expression may have the skill, the texture, the depth, and the durability of a work of art.

What the pioneering observers did not recognize quite so readily is that the existence of the pho graph has had a direct and identifiable effect on the remarkably rapid and widespread development of jazz idiom. Indeed, one might say that, above all others, jazz musicians have met the artistic challenge implicit in the existence of the phonograph in terms of both instrumental and stylistic development.

Every musician knows (and every critic should know) that there is no substitute for live performance. Yet it was not necessary for the younger musicians of the 1920s—those to whom the leadership ultimately fell in the 1930s—to have heard Louis Armstrong live in order to have absorbed, used, developed, made personal, or extended his remarkable innovations. Beginning in 1923, they heard him on recordings and learned him from recordings.

The New Orleans trumpeter Henry "Red" Allen, Jr., one of Armstrong's earliest followers, once patiently explained to an interviewer that it was not so much that they both came from the remarkable musical environment of the Crescent City: Allen had absorbed Armstrong's music from recordings—just like everybody else. And Allen, growing up in the days of the wind-up phonograph, had an opportunity not now generally available to younger musicians: he learned the music in all the keys simply by adjusting the old speed screw on the household's Victrola and playing along.

Such stories as Allen's might be repeated endlessly for every half-decade of the music, including the present one. And suffice it to say that anyone who makes any kind of sustained scholarly or critical statements about jazz and its history and development needs to know the recorded repertory, as much of it as possible and preferably all of it.

Indeed, there are obviously dangers for the scholar in not knowing the recordings and not acknowledging their power. I offer the following vignettes in evidence:

Recently in Washington a black pianist, professionally a maintenance man of the grounds at Howard University, was presented on Sunday morning television. He was there to play blues piano, and he was described as the carrier of an old and durable and important American musical tradition. He certainly was that. But there is one aspect of Afro-American life which many whites, many folklorists, and many jazz critics do not seem to realize—that is, that there is nothing very remarkable about a non-professional black man or woman playing blues piano for his own pleasure and self-enlightenment—nothing more remarkable than the ability of many a middle-aged white housewife to knock off "Humoresque" or Mozart's "Turkish March" as a result of girlhood piano lessons.

But to go back to our Howard bluesman: when he sat down to play, what came out was a reasonably respectable version of Avery Parrish's *After Hours,* a national hit throughout the 1940s for the Erskine Hawkins band and a piece that almost any pianist, amateur or professional, black or white, with an awareness of what was going on at that time in blues piano tried to learn. It seems to me that any discussion of what that Howard pianist was doing, and what he represents in cultural terms, needs to recognize and deal with the fact that he owes a major debt to the phonograph.

A second vignette. A number of years ago, a folklorist made a recording field-trip to the rural South. The results of his tapings were later released on commercial recordings with copious notes which, for the Negro music involved, spoke of the performers as isolated from the main highways and cultural currents, hence carriers of a "pure" and undefiled musical tradition. Blues performances in irregular choruses of twelve and one-half measures followed by eleven measures were seen as evidence of the fact that the blues was once a "spontaneous" and "free" form. Songs about trains inspired annotative passages about the meaning of railroads and travel in Afro-American life and in the blues tradition, etcetera.

Well, it happened that the folklorist had apparently not checked out the recent rhythm-and-blues hits before he undertook his field trip. Indeed, if he was like some folklorists, he probably scorned such music as a commercial corruption of a purer tradition. However, performer after performer on his recordings was clearly trying to imitate records that could be heard and enjoyed in the jukebox down at the crossroads tavern or in someone's record collection or on a local black radio station. In other words, the folklorist had recorded the efforts of amateurs to imitate the professionals they admired. As for the "irregular" blues choruses, they might well have been the result of simple musical inability. The following two pairs of recorded excerpts illustrate what I am talking about.

Example 1a: *Stop Breaking Down* (excerpt), performed by Forest City Joe (Atlantic LP 1352). Composer credit to Joe B. Pugh. Recorded in 1959.

Example 1b: *Stop Breaking Down* (excerpt), performed by Sonny Boy Williamson (Victor 20-3047). Composer credit to Sonny Boy Williamson. (However, this piece is in turn related to Robert Johnson's earlier piece of the same title.) Recorded on 19 October 1945.

Example 2a: *Drop Down Mama* (excerpt), performed by Fred McDowell (Atlantic LP 1352). Composer credit to John Estes; perhaps the title was researched by the record company. Recorded in 1959.

Example 2b: *Drop Down Mama* (excerpt), performed by Sleepy John Estes (Champion 50048). Composer credit to John Estes. Recorded on 17 July 1935.

A third vignette: As some of you know, in the 1940s there was an intense revival of interest in New Orleans jazz. On the positive side, it involved some interesting and important discographical, biographical, and critical work. On the negative side, it involved the critical position (which became prevalent in some intellectual circles) that the only authentic jazz, the only artistic jazz, was New Orleans jazz.

Some reputedly neglected but reputedly authentic artists were recorded during this period, and one such was clarinetist George Lewis. When Lewis said that his favorite clarinetist was Artie Shaw, his partisans were somewhat taken aback. But then, one could always retreat to the high ground that the artist is not necessarily the best judge of his own talent. When Lewis recorded a medium-tempo blues titled (by the record's producer) *St. Philip Street Breakdown,* some said that it was now possible for the listener to hear and take pleasure in an authentic, eloquent echo of New Orleans's glorious past. But alas, to anyone aware of the early 1940s recorded jazz repertory, Lewis was attempting to reproduc some ensemble figures from Woody Herman's *Chip's Boogie Woogie* and from Benny Goodman's (and Count Basie's) *Gone With "What" Wind*—and not doing so very well, I am obliged to add.

Example 3a: *St. Philip St. Breakdown* (first two choruses), performed by George Lewis (American Music LP 639). Composer credit to George Lewis. Recorded 27 July 1944.

Example 3b: *Chip's Boogie Woogie* (first chorus), performed by Woody Herman's Four Blue Chips (Decca 3577). Composer credit to Woody Herman. Recorded 10 September 1940.

Example 4a: *St. Philip St. Breakdown* (three-chorus excerpt) (as above).

Example 4b: *Gone With "What" Wind* (three-chorus excerpt), performed by the Benny Goodman Sextet (Columbia 35404). Composer credit to Count Basie and Benny Goodman. Recorded 7 February 1940.

Similarly, in praising trombonist Dickie Wells's solo on *Symphonic Scronch* in his excellent book *Jazz: Its Evolution and Essence,* André Hodeir did not know that it was largely based on Charlie Green solo from Fletcher Henderson's *The Gouge of Armour Avenue.* Hodeir had evidently not heard the Henderson record. Indeed, if he had, he might even have reinforced his praise of Wells, for although Wells largely reproduces Green's notes, the rhythmic nuances of his playing are instructively innovative for the instrument.

Example 5a: *Symphonic Scronch* (trombone solo by Dickie Wells), performed by Lloyd Scott and his orchestra (Victor 20495). Recorded in 1927.

Example 5b: *Gouge of Armour Avenue* (trombone solo by Charles Green), performed by Fletcher Henderson and his Orchestra (Vocalion 14859). Recorded 31 July 1924.

One final vignette, and with this one we are more directly in the domain of criticism and education rather than of scholarship. One of the most successful jazz ensembles in the United States is the Preservation Hall Band from New Orleans. The group does not produce hit records, but it does tour our cultural institutions, particularly our college campuses, year after year, and it is billed as an honorable preserver of a great tradition. Now, anyone who knows the music of Sidney Bechet or Jelly Roll Morton or King Oliver's Creole Jazz Band or Jimmy Noone or the early Louis Armstrong groups could not possibly agree with such a billing. Perhaps the average listener cannot discern that most of the Preservation Hall players are spirited amateurs, some of whom do not know their instruments, do not play in tune, and are putting on a show for white folks—who, alas, still view Afro-Americans and their music as exotics. But I do not think that an educator or music historian can allow himself such ignorance. And the answer for him lies in a knowledge of the recordings of Morton, Bechet, Oliver, and the rest.

Example 6a: *After You've Gone* (first 2 choruses), performed by Sidney Bechet (V-Disc 270). Recorded 8 December 1943.

Example 6b: *After You've Gone* (first chorus), performed by Bunk Johnson with George Lewis, Jim Robinson, et al (American Music LP 647). Recorded 3 August 1944.

David Baker

THE PHONOGRAPH IN JAZZ HISTORY AND ITS INFLUENCE ON THE EMERGENT JAZZ PERFORMER *

Perhaps I could fill in a few gaps concerning the phonograph and its influence on jazz—both deleterious as well as beneficent.

First of all, I think that a number of things about early recordings did in fact alter the flow of jazz. At the very beginning, the inability to record certain kinds of instruments—the string bass, for instance—in a proper manner seriously affected and attenuated the way the music developed. The

---

*Initially, Mr. Baker planned to speak on only the second of these matters. However, Martin Williams's paper having been read *in absentia,* Mr. Baker was asked to respond to it; the first portion of his remarks constitutes his response.

fact that the tuba hung around in jazz for a long time after it had outlived its usefulness, until roughly 1928-29, was largely due to the fact that technicians could not record a string bass properly. And I think that the drum set as we know it really came to full flowering much later than it might have, had it been able to be recorded properly. There were occasions when the drums were simply omitted. I think immediately of those marvelous duets by Earl Hines and Louis Armstrong, like *Weather Bird*: they might have used a drummer had it been possible to reproduce him adequately.

Another thing that the limitations of early recording equipment imposed on jazz was this: they often forced the soloist to function in a one-dimensional way. For instance, the inability to record certain nuances—the kinds of shadings that we think of as being part and parcel of every other kind of music—forced the jazz player in the beginning to play much the way boogie-woogie players did: loud, fast, and, in a word, one-dimensionally. I think that this has even carried over into many later players, simply because the tradition was established: you can hear an otherwise marvelous player stay at one dynamic level all the way through a piece, simply because "tradition" demands it. By extension, of course, that meant very often playing and functioning at a one-dimensional level as far as emotion went, too.

In the early days, too, it seems to me, the fact that "takes" could not be spliced meant that very often a jazz player who was told that he had to cut X amount of records in Y amount of time would simply let the mistakes go by. I think of one of the records of Louis Armstrong, with Lil Hardin playing in F major while the band is playing in F minor. I'm certain that when they listened back to the master, they probably recognized the mistake, but it was simply a question of economics—you didn't go back and re-record. And a lot of players, learning by imitation, imitated mistakes, simply because they didn't know they were mistakes. They sounded very hip and far out, perhaps.

Another thing that certainly has to be mentioned, in the relationship between jazz and recordings, is the three-minute versus the long-playing record. Jazz music took a very different direction once it was possible to record on LP. With the three-minute record, the solos were of great brevity (although it depended on the tempo: at a fast tempo, you obviously could play more choruses; at a slow tempo, you had to play less). This brevity, it seems to me, contributed to a lot of things. First of all, the solos were usually non-thematic, non-developmental, because playing thematically demand time for a solo to breathe. This was even commented on by critics, who must have thought that thematic development was something that jazz players couldn't handle, or that they simply did not think in developmental terms (which I don't believe at all). The solos were often concise, often to the detriment of musical logic. There was very little use of space, because when you've only got eight measure to play, you can't be interested in using space in an innovative or even intelligent way.

As a result, the musicians played very differently in a recording studio than they did in a club. I can remember going to hear Charlie Parker in 1948-49 and marvelling how he played in a live-perfor ance situation. Tom Owens has pointed this out, in his very excellent doctoral thesis on Parker. According to Owens, Bird tended to be more frivolous in live performance, using quotes in profusion and somehow not seeming to take things seriously. But I think that perhaps what Owens heard as fri olousness was instead Bird stretching out, being more imaginative, taking more chances. Similarly, when the long-playing record came in, jazz musicians started being more imaginative. Somebody wro that "beyond some point, every quantitative change will produce a qualitative change." With the LP, jazz solos had more time to breathe and could afford to be more discursive. The solo could unfold in a more epic way than on a three-minute record. (Now, it also led to some indulgences: we've all bee exposed to those solos that last twenty-four minutes on a record when there are only two minutes' worth of music.)

Jerry Coker points out, in his *Listening to Jazz,* that the LP record also put an extra burden on the player and that we lost a lot of audience because of it. He thinks that it was different when the points of recognition—the points of familiarity—were not so widely spaced. On a three-minute record, if it took forty seconds to play the head (the melody, that is—and everybody recognized the melody) and forty seconds to play the melody on the out-chorus, that didn't leave much in the middle to do. So you didn't lose the audience, because by the time they could get lost, the melody was back again. But with an eighteen-minute record that starts out in a very abstract way—say, something by John Coltrane—then you lose them in the middle, and they have to smoke pot or do something.

I think also that there tended to be a greater degree of conservatism when the record was brief. You can listen to Charlie Parker, who had one of the most inventive minds in the history of music, do three different takes on the Savoy recordings of *Now's the Time* or *Billie's Bounce,* and he plays essentially the same solo. Yet in live performances, you heard virtually nothing of the same content in replays of the same piece.

I also think the degree of subtlety was somehow affected by the shorter record. It's very difficult to be subtle when you haven't got much time. I can remember playing in big bands like Lionel Hampton's, and I'd sit there all night long, and I wanted to make an impression. I'd finally get eight measures. I'd run out there and try to play everything that was invented—you know, truncating ideas, crowding together too many ideas, and producing nothing but what one of my professors called "homeostasis."

With the advent of the long-playing record, a number of things happened. Even though it was already old by this time, the extended-chorus concept, where jazz musicians actually rival the best inventions of formal composers, could be heard on records. Someone like J. J. Johnson, playing a composition like *Jackie-ing* of Thelonius Monk, constructs a solo of such breathtaking beauty and conciseness and symmetrical proportions that it rivals virtually anything you would expect to hear in Bartók. And free forms and modality made their appearance—which they hadn't when the three-minute record was the point of reference. Modality, for all practical purposes, appeared around 1958, with the "Kind of Blue" album of Miles Davis, even though it probably had its beginnings with Miles's *Dear Old Stockholm,* with its long extended final section based on a modal scale.

I also believe that the diverse, pluralistic, pan-stylistic present world of the arts discussed by Leonard Meyer in his *Music, the Arts, and Ideas*—and by others—holds for jazz, too, and goes hand in hand with the LP and its effect on the dissemination of musical information. Records in general, but especially LPs, erase geographic and temporal provincialism. The thing that makes jazz such an exciting kind of music is perhaps its eclecticism and the fact that, as LeRoi Jones describes it, the minute a particular idea or concept is absorbed, then the people who created it don't deal with it anymore—they've gone somewhere else. Just as with language: where I live, they can tell how long I've been away from 25th and Martindale by the way I talk; if I come back referring to certain items with certain language, they know I've been away. In the same way, jazz loses its provincialism via the phonograph. Just as Bartók and Kodály and Holst and Dvořák and others tended to formalize and put limited regional folk idioms in a different framework, this happened also in jazz, primarily through the phonograph and the diffusion of recordings.

I also think that the phonograph has influenced the rate of style-change. One of the reasons why jazz sometimes seems so subject to fads, why it seems that so many kinds of movements ebb and flow, is that the phonograph makes it possible for these musics to reach a saturation point so quickly that the musicians just don't stay there any longer. That doesn't mean that one kind of music is any less important than another kind of music; it simply means that it changes more rapidly.

* * *

Now, let me approach all these matters from the standpoint of what I do for a living. I teach. I'd like to talk about the influence of the phonograph on the emerging jazz performer—specifically the young man or young woman who's in college or high school, learning jazz other than on the street

Anybody who's aware of what is happening in jazz today knows that almost every big band draws very heavily on the colleges for its personnel. I used to think that this was strictly an economic matter: you could get a young Indiana University musician for $125 a week, because he wanted to be with Woody Herman's band, whereas you had to pay $500 for a New York musician (he didn't necessarily want to be in Woody's band). But I don't think that that's all of it. I think the fact is that the phonograph—the awareness that comes through the phonograph—has given us musicians who function at a completely different level than the people who started out when I started out, way back when.

Look at Woody's band, Buddy Rich's band, the bands of Maynard Ferguson, Count Basie, Duke Ellington: they are full of college kids from Indiana University, from Berkeley, from the New England Conservatory, from the University of Utah, Miami University, the University of Illinois—it goes on and on. I think even more important than the players in these big bands is the influence of the young players on the small groups, where the changes really take place—the players who, for instance, are now in Max Roach's band or Art Blakey's or Horace Silver's. These young players, some of whom come from my university—like Randy and Mike Brecker, who are already pointing in some new direction—or from the University of Illinois—like Ron, Cecil, and Ron's ex-wife, Deedee Bridgewater—are in the vanguard of what's happening in music today. There are others, including students of mine like Freddie Hubbard, who have led the music in completely different directions. These are the people who are coming out of the colleges now. And if the teaching there is going on in any kind of meaningful way, it is ninety per cent under the influence of the phonograph, because that's what jazz is all about. Its history, as Martin Williams has pointed out, is inextricably bound to the phonograph. There was no other way: every performance of a jazz piece is *sui generis*, and the only way you can freeze it is on some kind of a recording.

Now, I'd like to deal specifically with my own programs and show you the pervasive influence of the phonograph in my training of the emerging performer. Traditionally, jazz, like all improvised musics, has been learned most efficiently through imitation. Before formal jazz education, all players learned their craft at the feet of their idols; in jam sessions and by listening to and playing along with recorded solos. The concept of *transcribing* such solos, as a method of learning, has immense value. In beginning one of my books, I talk about this:

> One of the undesirable consequences resulting from a surfeit of teaching methods, improvisation books, and other educational aids has been the virtual disappearance of the player who accelerates learning by playing along with records. It is lamentable that we teachers, authors, educators, and performers from the period before jazz method books

> have forgotten that we learned our craft by playing along with and studying the solos of our jazz heroes. While no rational educator would advocate a return to those times when recordings were the principal means of learning, it behooves us to reexamine the very important role that record transcriptions can and must play in the development and continued growth of jazz players.[1]

I go on to point out the analogy between learning a language and learning to play jazz, which is, in fact, another kind of language. And I point out the fact that the only way we can really cope with the myriad and sometimes violent developments in jazz is through the study made available to us by the phonograph record. The teaching of jazz improvisation, which is the *sine qua non* of jazz, depends almost totally on information gleaned from recordings. Whether it's my books or the books of George Russell, of Jerry Coker, of Dick Grove, or of whoever, all are predicated on the kinds of information that we get from recordings. None of us—no matter how many bands we played with or how much on top of it we think we are—really has enough deep knowledge of the entire jazz panorama to write a good theory book without studying records. When I began my first improvisation book (and each of the others, for that matter), it went like this: First, from surveying jazz histories and thinking about all the records that I had heard, I chose a number of the major figures in jazz—Louis Armstrong, Charlie Parker, Dizzy Gillespie, Stan Getz, and others. Then I listened to hundreds of records by these people to get a feeling for what was happening in the music. Then I consulted a Martin Williams or a Gunther Schuller, and my own empirical data, to decide which were the representative solos. I then transcribed the solos. Once the solos were transcribed, I analyzed them, finding the chordal patterns, the scales, the idiosyncratic things in each, and then I decided in what situations these things were used. And out of all this, I arrived at certain "rules." (That makes me a theoretician!) The point is that throughout the course of writing this theory book and then trying to teach from it, I was using phonograph recordings as my point of departure.

In fact, in each of my classes the phonograph is central. In my Styles and Analysis class, for instance, I tell the students their charge for the semester is to transcribe twenty solos of a single artist—say Charlie Parker or Dizzy Gillespie or John Coltrane. They then extract the language from those solos—those traits which seem to permeate them. For their class presentation, they choose four of those solos, for instance, and they take their instrument and play along with the recording while their transcription is shown on an overhead projector. I listen to see whether they're getting the inflections, and whether they're playing the correct notes. Then they analyze the solos, on the basis of a list of stylistic questions I have put together. It includes questions about such things as these: tune type (is it a ballad, a blues, a jazz original, a bebop tune? Latin? standard? free?); tempo; key; dramatic devices (slurs, rips, growls, glissandi); tessitura; scale patterns and preferences; recurrent motifs; performance practice (simple to complex structure? vertical or horizontal—chord-reference or thematic reference?); melodic construction (folklike melodies? bebop melodies? angular melodies?); and so forth.

The capper is this: after the student's presentation, I put a tune of *my* choosing, transcribed from a recording, on the blackboard. The student has ten minutes to come out of shock, collect his thoughts, and play the tune in the style of the musician he has analyzed. Now, it seems to me that's maximizing the potential of the phonograph as a teaching tool.

---

[1] David Baker, *Advanced Improvisation,* downbeat music workshop (Maher Publications, 1974), p. 26.

One thing I have noticed with amazement—and something I would claim to be definitely influenced by the phonograph—is the level of student jazz performances these days. Just one example: I recently heard a junior high school group in Eau Claire, Wisconsin, do *Central Park North* of Thad Jones and Mel Lewis, and do it in an absolutely authentic fashion—good solos, good everything. Why? First of all, they could buy the score (Thad and Mel and Stan Kenton and lots of others publish scores nowadays). But not only that: they could buy the recording and hear how the band played it.

With my own band at Indiana University, I carry it even further. We put on concerts with no music—no scores, that is. We learn everything from records. For a recent hour-and-a-half-long concert, I started rehearsals by putting on the recording of *Manteca* by Dizzy Gillespie and said, "All right band, everyone take his own part off that record." That first one took two hours; everyone was really scuffling, trying to get it. We got it. Then I put on *OW!!* by Dizzy Gillespie. That took twenty-five minutes. I put on *Jumping at the Woodside* by Count Basie: the second time around, they could play it; they were using their ears! And so on, through various records by Cannonball Adderley and other things we were to play on the concert. The concert was really hot; it was really beautiful. People couldn't imagine that you could make music without using scores.

Another area in which the phonograph plays a major role is that of "music minus one" records—especially some that a student of mine, Jamey Aebersold, has pioneered in making. These are stereo and have, for example, a bass recorded on one side and drums and piano on the other, and there's almost no leak-through from side to side. So, if you're a bass player, you can play together with a Ben Riley or a Kenny Baron; if you're a drummer, you can play with whoever is on the other side. Anothe set of these records presents single composers: the first one consists of Charlie Parker tunes, which yo can play with Kenny Baron and Ben Riley and Ron Carter backing you up. (You don't have to worry about the rhythm section getting uptight when you screw up.) These, it seems to me, provide an imaginative use of the phonograph as a teaching tool.

I've had a related idea (although I've found no takers yet among the record companies). That is to make a recording with the soloist recorded entirely from one microphone and the rhythm section from a different mike. Not only would the recording be a normal commercial item which would sell as such; it could also be used as a music-minus-one item by, for example, switching off the soloist and playing with the rhythm section, in an actual performance. Even better, have the solo transcribed, so that the transcription could be bought and played along with the soloist (or without him). That woulc be a very imaginative use of the phonograph, if only some company would get their act together and do it.

If I seem awfully excited about such things, I am! What I want to leave you with is this: If we are concerned with the pervasive influence of the phonograph and want it to be used for good, we would be well advised to concentrate in the area of education for performers: as someone has said, if you can influence the minds of young people, you can influence the flow and the direction of histor

---

AUDIENCE MEMBER: Mr. Baker, you seem to be advocating a revolutionary new pedagogy.

DAVID BAKER: Well, I think the phonograph took care of that. It did what Thomas Wolfe said you couldn't do: go home again.

AUDIENCE MEMBER: You talked about your improvisation books, then you talked about teaching your band without any charts. Are you beginning to distrust notation?

BAKER: No. I see notation as a tool, but not an end in itself. I have a friend who wrote a song that says, "Hey, little boy, sitting on the fence, put down your books; they're all in past tense." I think that that's a beautiful idea. I don't use the books I write, because by the time I get them published, usually in five months, I'm already somewhere else. Although I think that the basic truths are there and that they might provide some light for somebody, I also think they have to be seen as a means to an end. I can *reach* more people via books than I can reach otherwise. Hence I use books, but only as a means to an end.

CHARLES PRICE: What would you say about the importance of jazz students' being able to read music?

BAKER: Oh, I think it's absolutely indispensable. It's a fact of jazz life: when you go to play in a studio you don't have twenty hours to learn a piece, or even two. But, by the same token, I can do a lot to open ears with the phonograph that makes the students read better—makes them understand and perceive notation in a very different way than they might have otherwise.

Charlie Gillett

THE PRODUCER AS ARTIST

I'm a record producer, which is probably the most vilified figure in this conference. I have a record label in England, and so far I have been unsuccessful (which may make you like me better). Actually, that's not from my choice, however: my ambition is truly to have a top-ten hit single. (If it could be a top-ten hit single in this country—well, that's beyond ambition, just dreams.) So what I'm going to do, although it may be impossible, is to celebrate the record producer—specifically the record producer in the world of rock 'n' roll or pop music (terms that I will use interchangeably), since that is the world I work in, and the one I know best. My argument in this talk will be that the artist on a phonograph record can very well be the producer, not the performer. In much the same way that, in films, the film is the work of the director, and the star simply does what he is told by the director, so in music. This creates great resentment on the part of some people, both among the audience and among the performers, because they don't like the idea of someome dictating to them. But, to me, what matters are the intentions of the producer: if he has the interests of the performer and the audience at heart, he can benefit both of them by bringing them together (and, not so incidentally, sell a million records).

So, one by one, I would like to represent to you various kinds of record producers. You may be able to detect, incidentally, a common theme among the recorded excerpts that I have chosen, but I won't tell you what it is. Let me begin with an excerpt from a record that can stand for about the first fifty years of the record industry, as far as the nature and role of the producer is concerned:

Example: Frank Sinatra, *Three Coins in a Fountain* (Capitol 2816)

The producer we just "heard," the man who produced Frank Sinatra for Capital Records, was Voyle Gilmore. You may not have heard of him, and it doesn't matter too much if you haven't, because to me he was a typical sort of bureaucrat—a "fixer with a salary" is how I think of his type. All he had to do was to bring together the various components—a song written for a movie, an orchestra, an arrangement by Nelson Riddle, and a singer. I don't know how much such a producer thought about the audience; if he did think about it, it would have been in a rather cynical way ("They'll lap this one up!").

When Sinatra's *Three Coins* was produced, in the mid-1950s, there were five or six big record companies dominating popular music both here and in England. There was also an audience of young people in their teens (I was one of them) who didn't much go for this kind of music. They were itching to dance, and the records being made were not really very danceable. The question was: Is it worth it to worry about teen-age kids? The big companies thought: No, it isn't. But a few small companies—mainly in Los Angeles, Chicago, and New York—thought it was, and producers for these companies came to the rescue of the teen-agers. They made it their business to find artists, musicians, and songs that would suit an audience that wanted to dance.

Now, I think most of us tend to dismiss at any given time music which is made primarily for dancing. The more educated you get, somehow the more you can't stand pop dance music. I'm guilty of it at the moment, because I cannot stand what is currently called "disco" music. But I have a terrible feeling that in ten years' time whatever is going on then is going to make me feel that disco music was really good, because I certainly understand and appreciate the music which, if they'd had the term, they probably would have called "disco" music back in 1953. What they did call it was "rhythm-and-blues":

Example: Clyde McPhatter and the Drifters, *Money Honey* (Atlantic 1006)

Money Honey represents the product of a new kind of record producer whom I characterize as the "Renaissance man" in the industry. In New York, Ahmet Ertegun, the son of the Turkish ambassador, and a friend of his, a dentist named Herb Abramson—then, later another mutual friend, Jerry Wexler—put together Atlantic Records; it was Ertegun and Wexler who produced Clyde McPhatter and the Drifters. In Los Angeles, a man named Art Rupe ran Specialty Records from about 1945, and produced some very good records of, among others, Roy Milton. In Chicago, Leonard Chess started Chess Records and produced all sorts of great blues performers—Howlin' Wolf, Muddy Waters, and others.

These people, lacking the contacts or the expertise to get jobs with the major companies, started their own. Since black performers were resisted by the majors, they let the "Renaissance men" do wha they could. Most of these early independents had little musical background—Wexler and Ertegun are as musically untrained as I am—and they favored bandleaders who wrote their own material, rehearsed the own musicians, and left the producer to say, essentially, "Okay, let's go: start the machines," having made sure that the one mike they were using was in the right place to pick up everything. Nevertheless, these new producers, or at least a few whom I've mentioned, became genuine documentary recorders of great music, and specifically rhythm-and-blues.

By 1953 it was getting more complicated. The bands had run out of songs they could write them selves; they needed material written by other people. For the unmusical producer, the ideal thing was t get a songwriter to come along to the record session, to make sure that somehow his song got recorded more or less as he thought it should go (the producer also making sure that nobody got too drunk). Th next stage was to find an arranger or a song writer who could be trusted sufficiently to be left in the stu in charge of the production while the owner promoted the records to the DJ's or worked on their distribution. This gave several black musicians a chance to achieve prominent and influential positions in the creative process. Thus, Lew Chudd, owner of Imperial Records in Los Angeles, issued records made in New Orleans under the supervision of Dave Bartholomew, who worked with Fats Domino:

Example: Fats Domino, *Blue Monday* (Imperial 5417)

What happened in those days, if you were a songwriter, was that you would go to a record producer and, if you could persuade him to give you $15 for your song, you were very glad to walk away with the $15—and he had the song and put his name on the recording. For a long time, many of us thought that Dave Bartholomew was a fantastic songwriter: often, on the charts of the top hits, there would be "Lennon and McCartney" on top and "Domino and Bartholomew" just below them. But, actually, Domino and Bartholomew were just buying songs from all kinds of unknown people in New Orleans. Nevertheless, the songs they bought were good. A man at King Records in Cincinnati named Henry Glover, who also worked in New York, did a similar sort of thing.

I don't mean to sound flip about describing someone like Dave Bartholomew as ripping off songwriters: he himself was only paid a standard fee for work which should have at least deserved a royalty, if not a knighthood. So, while on the one hand a Dave Bartholomew has been unjustly praised for writing great songs, on the other hand the work that he did as a producer looking after Fats Domino (or looking after me as a dancer) was invaluable.

So an industry built up in the late '50s in this country, supplying teenagers with really good dance music under this sort of producer. A new kind of producer also came in—the songwriter who, instead of selling his song to a Dave Bartholomew, would say, if he was a strong enough character himself, "No, no, *I'm* going to go and produce that thing." Jerry Leiber and Mike Stoller were masters at this. Leiber is a brilliant songwriter, Stoller an accomplished pianist and arranger. They became more or less resident producers for Atlantic, making such terrific records as *Charlie Brown* and *Yakety Yak* (both in 1958). (Thus Wexler and Ertegun, although having the skill to go into the studio, recognized their level of musical accomplishment and, as standards went higher, found people who could be in greater musical control.)

The circle kept turning. The songwriter/producer could get his name on a record label, he could produce his songs so that they sounded the way he thought they ought to sound—but he was still vulnerable to record companies that did not pay fair producer royalties. The next step? Start a new record company of his own. This is what happened with one songwriter and arranger in Detroit. As a songwriter, he felt that his songs had been produced badly, so he became a producer. Then, having licensed his productions to record companies, he found he wasn't being paid adequately. Therefore he started his own label; he could now pay himself for his productions. Very significantly, the title of his first really big hit was *Money*:

Example: Barrett Strong, *Money* (Anna 1111)

Barrett Strong's *Money* set up Berry Gordy. I would call him the "New Renaissance Man." He really did do everything and I have nothing but admiration for him. As well as producing his own Motown records, Berry Gordy had an ear and an eye for talent that I don't think anybody in the popular business has ever had. He managed to find Marvin Gaye, one of the greatest singers ever, the Temptations, Martha and the Vandellas; also the extraordinary writers Holland-Dozier-Holland. They, Smokey Robinson, and Norman Whitfield also produced for Motown—in a workshop-cum-assembly-line manner that saw the producer as "factory foreman." Motown has been criticized for that. But listen to the records! Wonderful condensed energy . . . sometimes only two or three minutes, but minutes of absolute explosion—"lightning in a bottle" is Jerry Wexler's expression for it. People in America have never appreciated Motown records; it's to your shame that you haven't. It defies my understanding that there has not been one single book written in this country about Motown.

In England, people were astonished and excited by Motown. The do-it-yourself feel of their records inspired Britons to try something similar—more or less organic units of singers and other musicians who used the producers as expert advisers, at first mostly arrangers but later more often engineer The group that was first and most exciting along these lines was the Beatles:

Example: The Beatles, *Can't Buy Me Love* (Capitol 5150)

The interesting thing about the Beatles was that they seemed to be in control of their own records; they seemed to do everything themselves. Nobody's ever been quite sure whether that was true They recorded in England for EMI records, and there was a man called George Martin who was listed as producer of everything they ever did with EMI. But the mystery has always been: what did George Martin actually do? Did he advise them? Did he make the tea? It could have been almost nothing or it could have been a lot. That's often true of a producer: his role can be very enigmatic and unclear. I've watched people producing records, and sometimes I'm not really sure what they're doing. Somebody else is the man who controls the tape recorder—the engineer—and if an arrangement is needed, an arranger is brought in. So what is that man sitting in the corner doing? I say the Beatles seemed to do everything themselves: they were very bright people; Lennon and McCartney did write the song they went onstage or on TV and they all played the instruments themselves; they sounded very much as they had sounded on records. Therefore, presumably they produced themselves. But I have my doubts—I think George Martin probably was at least some sort of a diplomat and psychologist, arbitrator and referee between the conflicting intentions of Paul McCartney, who was a relatively conservative figure in the group, and John Lennon, who probably tended to be an adventurously uncommerci one.

Whether or not the Beatles were their own producers we'll never know. But they gave the performers more credibility as artists in popular music than ever before, and inspired most of what has happened since. They created a model, and other people who followed definitely *were* their own producers. First it was white bands here—the Buffalo Springfield group comes to mind—then others here and in England. Of course, producers in the old-fashioned sense were by no means entirely eliminated the name of Richard Perry, for example, as producer of Carly Simon and an album by Ringo Starr, is prominently featured on record jackets, and clearly he is an invaluable figure. But in the same period many artists have taken over in the studio, usually after a period of working with a producer.

As artist control has increased, however, so has studio technology. Greater expertise in this area has become necessary, as the process of recording itself has become more complicated. The importanc of "effects" in the over-all sound has increased; thus, so has the importance of the engineer—or the producer as technician. But, more than ever, records are potentially under the control of the artist: the artist is producer, the producer becomes an artist. Here we arrive at some sort of high point of the art of making records:

Examples: Marvin Gaye, *Inner City Blues* (Motown M9-791; Pink Floyd, *Money* (Harvest SMAS-11163)

The production of both of those recordings was under the complete control of the artists. The record companies agreed to pay for the studio time and put out whatever tape was brought to them. In the context of the whole commercial recording industry, you must agree that it's quite unusual for an artist to have such control over what he does, especially considering the financial stakes involved. And the real point to me is that the art is not invalidated by the way it was made nor by the fact that it is so successful.

Finally, really coming back almost to where we started: The ultimate way for the artist to have really complete control is to go onstage and record a live LP, with the engineer obliged to do nothing but record what the artist does, document what happens, then to go back with the tapes—you've seen these gigantic sixteen- or twenty-four-track things—mix them down, even cheat a little by overdubbing corrections, and make sure that the way it finally sounds is how the artist wants it. This is literally a development of the last two or three years, when recording equipment has become so good that we can get from onstage recording sound-quality that is as good as in the studio.

Example: Ry Cooder, *How Can a Poor Man Stand Such Times and Live* Warner Bros B-3059)

That was Ry Cooder retrieving a song first recorded in 1928 by a man called Blind Alfred Reed. Now, Ry Cooder—who is not perhaps in the same category as the other artists I've mentioned since he isn't that successful, but is a particular favorite of mine—is a middle-class Californian who has had none of the experiences about which he sings. Nevertheless, as performing producer or producing performer (but either way, as some kind of all-round artist), he is in control of the recording. He doesn't get just any old studio musician to play accordion with him; he gets Flako Jimenez, a 45-year-old Tex-Mexican. He finds real gospel singers in California to sing with him. He uses an earlier record for his material. And then in performance, he imposes his own vision on all of this—the artist as final, total producer in control of his own recording.

CHARLES PRICE: About live recordings and the artist being in control: Many live recordings produced by someone other than the artist are better than those the artist produces himself. Live recordings take a special kind of production sense; they have to be just as carefully produced as studio recordings. The opposite side of that coin is that studio recordings can end up being better "live performances" than live performances, if that magic that can happen is not lost in the production procedure. Also, I think it's naive to think that live performances are somehow *truer* than studio performances: it's no longer a question of just putting a microphone up there.

CHARLIE GILLETT: O.K. Absolutely. Not only have I been a slave of records all my life, but only occasionally have I truly enjoyed an entire live performance. You have to sit down in a lot of these places, which is insane to have to do with popular music. Also, people smoke and it gets in your eyes, and so forth. I didn't mean to imply by playing Ry Cooder live at the end that I was recommending a live performance as being the definitive popular music record—far from it. It's very rare that a live-performance record is good. So I don't argue with you at all.

AUDIENCE MEMBER: The difference between a live performance and a studio performance—the technical difference—would be the use of splicing or multiple-track non-synchronous recording, I think.

When these are introduced, from the conceptual point of view there's no more performance. Fourteen different performers coming in, each laying down his track while hearing the others on tape—well, they are making a medley of contributions, but the notion of *performance* is without meaning.

GILLETT: Would you follow through on that and say that a film is an invalid dramatic thing because its last scene was shot first?

AUDIENCE MEMBER: I think you have to know what you're listening to in order to make aesthetic sense of it. I judge the product by the process. I have to know how the thing was made, in order to know what it is and how to tell what its qualities are.

GILLETT: Well, that's what education does to us, and I'm sorry for you. It nearly got me the same way.

AUDIENCE MEMBER: I wonder whether the "artist as self-producer" phenomenon of pop music is becoming more common in other types of music, and, if so, whether it has different meanings. The reason I ask this is because it *is* happening more in classical music, but there it has a completely different function, as a kind of "vanity press" for composers. If he can't get recorded any other way, he finds the money somehow and takes his tape to certain record companies—everybody knows which ones they are—and the companies will issue them.

WILLIAM FERRIS: Well, that's been going on since records began. James Thomas, the blues artist, gave me a recording he cut as a teenager in Yazoo City. It's a little plastic disc: one could go into a booth, like the ones where you have yourself photographed, and cut your own record. It's still going on, especially now that cassette recorders are so widespread. What's interesting is that when a folklorist works with an artist, often the artist will notice very carefully what the folklorist is interested in—the types of performances, traditional or more contemporary. Then, after the folklorist leaves, the musician will make his own recordings and circulate them in the community on a cassette.

DAVID BAKER: In the jazz area it's also happening, mostly by people who already have some production expertise. For instance, on Cannonball Adderley's last two albums, "The Phoenix" and "Lovers," Cannonball is listed as producer. Of course, he had been cutting records for twenty years; he was astute; he had found out how it's done.

GILLETT: I think it's relevant that he had been doing it with other people for twenty years and finding out what to do. Anybody who's a writer can tell you the value of a good editor. The ideal editor is the one you think hasn't done anything to your writing, and only later do you find out that he did all sorts of things. That is equally what a good producer does. The artist feels helped; he doesn't feel there's anything getting in the way.

AUDIENCE MEMBER: Mr. Gillett: about the artist being a producer now—do you think this would happen for long if they didn't make money for the record company?

GILLETT: No. But, on the other hand, Ry Cooder has made very little money for anybody. He's now [1977] on his sixth or his seventh LP for Warner Bros. only Reprise and, as far as I'm concerned, to their great credit they have supported him without his making much money for them. I think the record business is unjustly criticized by people who assume that its every move is engendered by this terrible word "money."

RICHARD CRAWFORD: I'd like to know what the sequence of your recorded examples means.

GILLETT: Oh, it's just that they were all about money.

V

THE PHONOGRAPH AND THE SCHOLAR AND CRITIC

Scholars and critics of music perform related, if not identical, tasks, and one session of THE PHONOGRAPH AND OUR MUSICAL LIFE included as panelists two scholars and two critics. One of the scholars, Charles Hamm, is particularly identified with research into Western art-music, and also American popular music; the other, William P. Malm, is an ethnomusicologist who specializes in non-Western music. (Professor Malm's paper, which relied for its impact on accompanying recorded examples, is not included here.) One of the critics, John Rockwell, is a newspaper writer; the other, David Hamilton, is a magazine music editor. The session was introduced and chaired by yet another scholar, Richard Crawford, who specializes in American music.

Richard Crawford

INTRODUCTION

Recorded sound, our reactions to it, and our uses of it help to reveal a particular aspect of our culture's genius—what we might call a genius for transposition. With the help of the phonograph, we are now able to remove music from the setting in which it originated and to call it back and hear it just about anywhere and at any time we like. And so skillfully has this miracle been accomplished that few even notice or suspect that anything noteworthy has occurred. We can experience, in succession, the sound of *Die Götterdämmerung,* or Machaut's Mass (perhaps composed for the coronation of a French king more than 600 years ago), or a Venda initiation dance from Africa, and give no more thought to the means by which the sound reaches us than to the facts that the room in which they are heard is lighted with electricity and centrally heated. One measure of the impact of recorded sound upon our musical life is that, for most of us at least, the idea of recorded sound has no impact at all. We have trouble imagining a musical world without it. Similarly, we accept as normal the circumstance that we enjoy access to music from distant ages and corners of the world, and we are not much given to thinking about what these transpositions might mean.

Most of us accept music as a means of making artistic statements and of stimulating aesthetic experience. The recording supports and reinforces that function by preserving such statements. At the same time, it changes them. One aspect of that change is that the recording tends to reduce the musical statement to the sound alone, to proclaim that the only real significance of a piece of music lies in its sound, and that its original context is unimportant. But what do we mean when we say "original context?" First, we mean the social-cultural context in which the music was originally created and performed. That context involves the relationships between creators and performers and auditors, the purpose for which the music was created and the function it was expected to serve, and the customs and experiences and social organization of that society. Original context also means, secondly, the physical and temporal circumstances for which the performance was intended—the kind of space that the music was to fill, the physical arrangement of the performers and the audience, perhaps even the time of day. Thirdly, original context also means—and here we come closer to the things that scholars and critics of Western art music are likely to ponder—the context of musical performance prac tice: the identity of the performers and the degree of their training, the sound ideal they favored (as shown by their instruments and their singing technique), the way in which performance was related to notation, the spirit in which performers approached the music they were to perform.

These are just a few of the things that might be meant by "original context." To recount them is immediately to notice how remote from the essence of music they seem to most lovers of music, including musicians. Just naming some of the elements of musical context confirms that recording reinforces our tendency to focus on musical sound at the expense of context, to define music solely on the basis of its sound. It is even possible that the accessibility of recorded music might inhibit a search for context. If a piece of music can make its impact purely from its sound surface, most listeners will have no reason to inquire further. Recordings from what used to be called "exotic" cultures often come with explanatory notes and pictures; this implies a belief that the music may be misunderstood unless some context is provided. But many recordings of Western classical music reflect a different belief. By depicting in a dramatic pose, for example, the conductor of an orchestra on a recording, and by carrying only gossipy or discursive remarks on the jacket, they seem to proclaim that the sound-surface is self-sufficient. On the other hand, recordings of popular music of the last two decades carry lavish statements on context, often in the form of pictures. Information about the performers of such recordings also appears in other media (radio, film, TV, the press), which helps to establish the music as an emanation of a whole life-style. Certainly the sound of popular music is of primary importance, but the marketing of popular recordings as not just songs, but complete cultural statements, irrevocably bound up in understood contexts, helps to explain the enormous power and influence of recent popular music. (To take just a single aspect of that influence, one could argue that pop and blues recordings have been the primary contact point for many white Americans with the culture of black Americans—especially with blacks' language and their attitudes toward life. If you share my belief that our history has no social issue more significant than the relationship between blacks and whites, the phonograph has played a powerful role indeed in shaping the quality and content of our social lives.)

Music in recorded form lends itself to other purposes than that of making artistic statements. For example, on the practical level, recorded music is an ideal medium for transmission and instructio To suggest just a few instances:

1. The Suzuki method teaches young children to play instruments by listening to others play, and requires the students to own and play recordings of Suzuki pieces, thus introducing a whole gen eration of youngsters to the direct power of the phonograph as an aural model.
2. The phonograph has always been an important force in the transmission of jazz, allowing player to penetrate deep into the styles of original improvising soloists such as Louis Armstrong, Charli Parker, and Miles Davis. (Note the early New Orleans trumpet player Freddie Keppard, who refused to record because he didn't want anybody stealing his licks.)
3. Performers of "classical" music are likely to be very familiar with the recorded performances of their predecessors and contemporaries, and to learn from them.
4. Scholars and players of folk music tell of circular processes of oral transmission, whereby educated musicians who have learned songs via recordings go into the field and introduce traditional performers to these versions.

5. Teachers of music appreciation and history find the phonograph indispensable, and most would be lost without it.

In these practical uses of recorded music, a different kind of transformation has taken place. When a musical performance is offered as an artistic statement, it is an end in itself. But if a musical performance is recorded, it invites further use and can no longer be an end. The transforming of ends into means toward further ends gives them new meanings, focusing on their anatomy rather than on their surface and making them sources for technical and historical study—links in a chain of utilitarian purpose.

Current musicological training teaches would-be scholars that their goal is to extend knowledge—to broaden or deepen what we already know about music. I would take the task of the critic to be something quite different: to interpret experience—to engage in a musical experience such as listening and to communicate to an audience one's idea of what that experience has meant. A topic like the present one asks the scholar to take on something akin to the critic's function, and that might make us uneasy; scholars tend to be more at home digging in the archives than interpreting their experience (especially in public). The phonograph occupies a pervasive, even central, position in our lives, but few of us have given it much thought. The proverb that seems to apply here is: if you want to understand the nature of water, don't ask a fish.

A fish may lack perspective on the meaning of the water in which he swims, but his experience of it gives him life and defines his existence. To jump as fast as possible out of this stream of thought, I believe that the scholarly-critical perception of the phonograph has focused almost exclusively upon the *experience* that it provides, leaving the understanding of the nature of that experience to chance. Musical scholars, and perhaps critics too, share the priorities of our musical culture as a whole. The phonograph provides almost unlimited opportunities for experience—for listening to music—and radio stations, academic courses, textbooks and other writings, record jackets, and other agencies and media give us bits and pieces of context that help us to understand some things about that experience. But, so far as I have been able to discover, "our musical life" provides no philosophy or unifying framework for helping us to get at the meanings of this multiplicity and contradictoriness of sound experience in which we revel every day. We share a faith that experience is, in and of itself, a good thing—the more the better—and that perhaps somewhere down the road, at least some of us may receive fleeting glimmers of understanding. If we don't, at least it's been fun. (And has it ever been fun! . . .)

Our landscape is filled with music, chiefly because recorded sound makes music available, cheaply. So far, the response of musicians, including scholars and critics, has been to accept that condition gratefully and, at least in the case of scholars, to bend their efforts to add to the profusion. Perhaps a conference like this one signals that we might be prepared to risk losing our innocence. But a loss of intellectual innocence would be no threat at all to our musical innocence. Music is too powerful for that.

John Rockwell

THE PHONOGRAPH AND THE MUSIC OF TODAY

I would like to begin with a personal attestation to the phonograph in *my* life. My musical upbringing involved some industrious if not overwhelmingly talented assaults on the piano, some music theory and history courses in college, plus a lot of concert-going experience. But one determining factor in my commitment to be involved with music in my life was the phonograph. In my mid-teens I fell into the habit of collecting records, at that time almost exclusively of classical music, although I had been avocationally involved in pop music as a younger child. It was the experience of walking down to a store in the small town of Andover, Massachusetts, and buying Western musical culture on records that more or less determined what I was going to be really interested in, in my life.

It never occurred to me, and it still really doesn't, to be concerned or embarrassed by the fact that I was listening to records rather than live music. Virgil Thomson told me recently that, far from crushing musicality, the phonograph has been an enormous boon to it, his theory being that technical evolution spurs things on rather than quenching them—and I agree with him on that. There are certai *derrière-gardistes* who are terribly concerned about the morality or ethics or purity of electronic musi too. Their position seems absurd to me: of course there's nothing wrong with electronic music; it's a tool like any other. Similarly, for people to worry that the phonograph is somehow inhibiting to natural musicality strikes me as almost equally absurd. On the contrary, it's obviously helpful. The ques tion is: in what way is it a help, and in what possible future ways can it be a help?

In my own case, far from discouraging me to go to live concerts, becoming interested in phonograph records was the spur to start going to them, and I went to them—and still do go to them —with a manic quality that appalls people. So, if there was an element of worry in the basic theme of this conference, a fear that there might be something wrong with the phonograph in our musical life, I'm not one to reinforce that worry.

The remarks that I would now like to make address themselves essentially to the question of the role the phonograph has played in altering critics' or scholars' perceptions of the music of today. Essentially, what I think the phonograph has done (and in itself this is not a particularly revelatory remark) is simply to have made available to us . . . everything. (At least, everything if one chooses to pursue it.) Those who are interested don't have to go to Indonesia any more to hear Indonesian musi they can hear it on records. If Professor Crawford, in his remarks about "context," was hinting that the availability of, say, a gamelan record tends to lessen everybody's interest in going to Indonesia, or experiencing Indonesian dances or shadow-plays or whatever, that is clearly not true. Clearly, the existence of these records has done exactly the reverse: it has spurred ethnomusicological studies in the Western world; it has vastly increased our knowledge of and interest in not only the music of the East but its context as well.

What I am saying is that the phonograph has made available a vast range of music to those who are interested in encountering it. Now, if you do encounter this vast range, you inevitably gain a who new perspective on the music of your own culture. And what such a confrontation can do is to make one realize—give one a kind of enlightened conception of—the relativity of rules in music, and make one understand that the basic forms of Western music are not necessarily handed down from on high. The scale-patterns of Western music, whatever sense they make and whatever values they may have had, are relative. The rhythmic patterns of Western music are not only relative but somewhat primitive. Notions of timbre have evolved in certain specific socio-cultural ways in the West; they are only one of many possibilities. An awareness of these possibilities has led, and is leading, to a change in the way that we in the West make music. And I think—being essentially a Polyanna in nature—that this is a very healthy thing, even if it does mean that people are puzzled in concert halls now, at concerts of new music.

I want to add some remarks about popular music and the phonograph. It seems to me that the popular musician, rather more than the classical musician, has seized upon the potential of making a music the aesthetic of which is defined by the possibilities of the recording studio. A couple of years ago a brouhaha developed when Columbia Records was trying to peddle the idea of "surround sound," and conductors like Pierre Boulez recorded perfectly innocent pieces of classical music and put the trumpets and drums behind you (just for the hell of it, as far as I could see: fine and good to clarify polyphonic textures, but please!). That brouhaha was interesting because it underlined the absurdity of having to trick up perfectly honorable works composed in one aesthetic just because there didn't seem to be any way of producing interesting *new* works that actually capitalized on the technology.

In popular music, there's no such problem. People are perfectly happy to have one person overdub a whole symphonic-sounding rock record, or to have a whole genre—disco—which evolves out of electronic sounds of one kind or another, or to perfect ways of playing a synthesizer in a perfectly natural, vital, and interesting way (as Stevie Wonder has done) that has defined a whole genre of black music. This is not to speak of the more overt and experimental progressive rockers, like Brian Eno, who lap very much over into the avant-garde. It seems to me that in our record stores, mixed in among all sorts of obvious *Dreck,* a whole musical culture is taking shape and happily prospering, totally independent of the attention of most scholars and critics, and that, although the music won't necessarily profit from their attention, they themselves might well profit from lending it some attention.

Charles Hamm

THE PHONOGRAPH AS TIME-MACHINE

I'm going to talk basically about Stephen Foster. Let me begin by playing a fairly recent recording of Foster's *Come where my love lies dreaming* by the Robert Shaw Chorale. The piece was written by Foster—exceptionally for him, as a quartet, not as a solo song with piano accompaniment. The performance by the Shaw Chorale is technically accurate: they sing the music as published; it's not arranged; they sing it note-for-note the way Foster wrote it down.

Example: Stephen Foster, *Come where my love lies dreaming;* performed by the Robert Shaw Chorale (RCA LSC-2295)

As you could hear, this is beautiful, accurate, useful for us in teaching about Stephen Foster or in doing research, if we wish to transform into sound the published music of Foster. That, incidentally, is the theme of my remarks, more than Foster himself: the fact that as a result of the phonograph scholars and students now have access to the actual sound, as opposed to notes written on paper, of almost the entire span of Western art music. We can now deal with it as sound and not just as symbol.

What we heard was a good performance, but I think it is one that says more about the Robert Shaw Chorale, and about the mid-twentieth century, than it does about Stephen Foster. I'm sure you recognize that this chorus can pick up another piece of music—a motet by Palestrina, say, or the Monteverdi *Vespers*—and sing it in pretty much the same way, that is, with the same type of vocal production, the same precision, the same concentration on exact intonation and phrasing and dynamics.

There is another dimension, of course, to what the phonograph has done for us. In addition to making it possible for us to hear modern performances of any music which has been notated, it has made it possible for us to go back a certain distance in time, in the direction of hearing performances from the very period of the music we are dealing with. Let me play you another recording of the same Foster song as sung by John McCormack. McCormack was not a contemporary of Stephen Foster, of course, but he is about as close as we can get to Foster with sound recordings. Now, as you will hear, McCormack does the song very inaccurately: it was written for quartet, and McCormack sings it as a solo; the choral part has been condensed as an instrumental accompaniment. Many scholars would say, "We can't use this recording of *Come where my love lies dreaming* because it's not right; the performance forces are all wrong."

Example: Foster, *Come where my love lies dreaming;* performed by John McCormack on *Because and Other Songs of Sentiment* (RCA VIC-1622)

There are obviously enormous differences between McCormack's performance and that of the Shaw Chorale. Most of them could be summarized by saying that McCormack is singing the Foster song in an operatic way. Stephen Foster sung operatically? Well, in fact, the McCormack recording reminds us of some things that the Shaw recording does not: that Foster knew Italian opera; that he transcribed pieces by Donizetti (in his instrumental collection, *The Social Orchestra*); that, if we can believe his brother Morrison, he studied music of opera composers at night, looking at scores and copying them; and that he and Morrison were friendly with an opera singer in Cincinnati named Madame Biscacciati and the three of them went together to performances. (Morrison does not specify which performances, but they were undoubtedly performances of operas, and at that time the operas must have been Italian.)

If we are reminded of those things, and can forget all the false statements that have been made about Foster's musical background (that he heard blacks singing as a child, that his music reflects the sounds of the plantation, etc.), then we are pointed in the right direction—a more correct direction, I think, than that indicated by the Shaw Chorale, and one which, if pursued, will lead us to the interesting fact that Stephen Foster not only knew Italian opera and loved it but wrote it. This song has whole chunks of Italian opera in it. It's difficult for us to hear it that way because we know it as a "Stephen Foster song," and we have to make an abrupt turn to try to think of it as an Italian operatic song. But if we quite carefully identify the stylistic traits of Italian opera—its melodic style, its treatment of the voice, and other things—and then look at certain Foster songs and find the same traits, we begin to see Foster in a different perspective from the one that has been presented to us by most (not all) scholars of Foster's music.

This is one obvious demonstration of the value that older recordings can have for us, as opposed to more recent ones. If we wish to use the phonograph as an aid to scholarship, by dealing with the music as sound, we can now go back almost a hundred years. We can't, of course, go back farther than that. We cannot listen to recordings of Liszt playing the piano, nor can we hear the Papal Choir in the sixteenth century singing music by Palestrina. Thus when I say that it is now possible for a scholar or a student to hear, on recordings, music from the whole range of Western cultural history, I must qualify that by adding that, for most of the period, we are listening to the music as interpreted by someone from a later time.

Let me now take what may seem at first to be a rather different direction. I've been much involved recently with music in the oral tradition. Since by definition music in the oral tradition has no notation, our first-hand knowledge of it differs a great deal from that of art music. We can reconstruct, in sound, art music for many centuries back; we can go back, through recordings, only about a hundred years into the past of music in oral tradition. However, I am going to try to suggest that the apparent dichotomy between the two kinds of music may not in truth be a real one. I am going to suggest the possibility that the sound of earlier music in oral tradition has not been lost and that perhaps we can deal, in sound, with music in oral tradition from the nineteenth century, or the eighteenth, or the seventeenth—even though there was no one around at the time to make recordings of it.

Let me go back to Stephen Foster for a moment and play you a recording, again by the Robert Shaw Chorale, of a different type of Foster song—a minstrel song:

Example: Foster, *Oh! Susanna;* performed by the Robert Shaw Chorale (RCA LSC-2295)

You will have recognized that here we have, not anything like the original Foster song, but an arrangement. The question is: how can we determine what minstrel songs sounded like in Stephen Foster's day? How, in other words, can we reconstruct a song like *Oh! Susanna* the way Foster might have imagined it, in sound?

There is a great deal of evidence about performance practice among early minstrel-show troupes. We have illustrations that show the instrumentation of the bands; we have sheet-music covers depicting the bands in action; we have many written accounts of the shows; we even have some descriptions of the sound. These can serve as our starting point. Minstrel bands, during Foster's early years as a composer of minstrel-show music, normally used one or two banjos, a fiddle or two, and percussion instruments (bones, a tambourine, perhaps some other instruments) along with singing. That was the makeup of the minstrel troupe until well along in the nineteenth century. Now, to my knowledge there are no recordings, even from the very late years of the century, of minstrel troupes with this instrumentation which we might take as samples of the sound of the minstrel band in the early and mid-nineteenth century. If we wish to hear the sound, then, we must proceed in another way.

In addition to the pictorial and descriptive evidence that I have mentioned, there are such other tools as banjo tutors—instruction books that preserve in notation the types of music that banjos played. Hans Nathan worked with this evidence in preparing his book on *Dan Emmett and the Rise of Early Negro Minstrelsy.* In a chapter discussing the minstrels' instruments and their methods of performance, he came up with this description of the sound of a minstrel band:

> There were no chords in the ensemble because the banjoist played only a melody; this is evident from banjo methods of the fifties which also described an older practice. They show in addition that the banjoist liked to vary the main melody by inserting into it the open tones of his two highest strings. . . . The fiddler may have played the tune straighter than the banjoist, though with occasional variants including dotted notes and syncopations, and with open strings as drones, as is still the custom in the backwoods. . . . The volume of the minstrel band was quite lean, yet anything but delicate. The tones of the banjo died away quickly and therefore could not serve as a solid foundation in the ensemble. On top was the squeaky, carelessly tuned fiddle. . . . The sound of the band . . . was scratchy, tinkling, cackling, and humorously incongruous.

(I don't understand the last phrase, but those are Nathan's words.) Then, on the basis of this chapter on performance, Nathan went ahead to do something which I think is fascinating, but which has received almost no attention: he took several minstrel tunes and scored them, not following "artistic dictates" but following his conclusions about the way the music would have been played in Emmett's time.

We know that the instruments in the early minstrel bands were those of music in oral tradition of the time, and we know that even today there are banjo players and fiddlers playing traditional Anglo-American music. It has been proved beyond any question, I think, that most of the early minstrel songs were not composed but were adapted; that Dan Emmett himself, and most of the early minstrel composers, simply took what must have been traditional Anglo-American tunes and adapted them to the minstrel band, fitting words to them—that their songs were, in fact, arrangements. Now, it so happens that if we look around we can find, to the present day, groups of musicians with precisely the same instrumentation as that of the early minstrel troupes. Furthermore, if we recall Hans Nathan's description of the minstrel band's sound, we find that it describes precisely some of this music that is played today. Let me play you a piece recorded by a group called the Iron Mountain String Band. The instrumentation is banjo and fiddle; later on, a voice enters. There is no harmony, no chords; the banjoist is playing a melody and hitting some of the open strings to form a sort of rhythmic and melodic ostinato. The banjo and the fiddle are playing in unison, not in parts, and when the singer enters, he is singing the same melody.

Example: *Cluck, old hen;* performed by "Banjo" Bill Cornett on *The Iron Mountain String Band An Old Time Southern Mountain String Band* (Folkways FA 2473)

I submit that this is the sound of the minstrel band, and that it has not been lost. By locating a record of a group like this, we have the actual sound of a minstrel band. Moreover, the phonograph has not killed this music: performers such as these are not scarce; there are probably more people playing music like this now than there were twenty or thirty years ago. Some of the musicians learn from records, but the tradition is not being lost as a result; it is resisting the phonograph record. (But that's the wrong way of putting it; it is benefiting from the phonograph record.)

Let me play you another piece, from an album called *Mountain Music of Kentucky.* Incidentally, the album jacket carries a photograph of a gentleman in ordinary clothes, with a banjo, who, from lithographs and other pictorial evidence we have from the minstrel-show days, could well be a performer in a minstrel troupe, except that his face is not blackened. This is a song called *Blackeyed Susie,* with the same instrumentation as *Cluck, old hen.* I submit that it is close in melodic style and many other ways to *Oh! Susanna*—and with the authentic sound.

Example: *Blackeyed Susie;* performed by Roscoe Holcomb on *Mountain Music of Kentucky* (Folkways FA 2317)

Now let me take the next step. First I'll play you just a fragment of a piece called *Buck Creek girls*—the introduction to it, which is played by a banjoist. You'll hear that the banjoist is playing a pentatonic melody on the middle strings, and striking the other open strings in a rhythmic and melodic ostinato.

Example: *Buck Creek girls;* performed by "Banjo" Bill Cornett on *Mountain Music of Kentucky* (Folkways FA 2317)

Now, without identifying it, I'll play you another piece.

Example: *Gitari Na Congo;* performed by Bakia Pierre on *The Music of Africa Series; Musical Instruments I. Strings* (Kaleidophone KMA-1)

I think that anyone who can't hear what's going on doesn't deserve to hear! It is of course an African piece. I think that the link, in sound, between the African banjo-like instrument and the nineteenth-century American derivative of it is perfectly audible. We can hear what happened: not only was the instrument—or at least the concept of the instrument—brought over from Africa, and similar instruments constructed by slaves, which then became models that were taken over by whites, but an important part of the musical vocabulary of the African instrument was maintained—the single melody on some strings, with the other strings being strummed as an ostinato. I have been amazed to find in Vermont and New Hampshire literally hundreds of people still playing banjo in this style, and singing to this type of accompaniment. They offer beautiful examples of the blending of African and American cultures in a style that dates back to a time earlier than such a blending has been thought to have occurred (because I have no doubt that this type of music was being made even in the eighteenth century).

I'll end with a simple image. I think that the phonograph gives the scholar a time-machine. Through the phonograph we can zoom back in time to the seventeenth century or the thirteenth century, or whenever, and experience in actual sound the music that we are concerned with. It may be an appalling parallel, but it is as if an American historian could turn this way and see the Battle of Gettysburg in progress, then turn that way and hear George Washington giving a speech. It seems to me that since we do have this wonderful time-machine (although there are some problems with it, as I have suggested) the fact that some scholars refuse to deal with it—with music as sound, in other words—is totally inexcusable.

AUDIENCE MEMBER: Apropos of Stephen Foster and opera: His songs were widely sung by the great singers of the nineteenth century. When people like Adelina Patti toured the country, what did they sing by way of American songs? Stephen Foster. What's more, they recorded them: we have Foster recordings by Patti and Nellie Melba, and even Emma Calvé singing *The Old Folks at Home.* The McCormack approach, then, is appropriate in another way—as part of the singers' tradition.

JOHN ROCKWELL: However fat and fruity and white-bread Protestant the Robert Shaw singers and their arrangements may sound to us, they constitute their own tradition. Even if they don't sound like Stephen Foster's minstrels, they sound like themselves; they're part of their own tradition.

CHARLES HAMM: I agree completely. I didn't intend to give any other impression.

David Hamilton

SOME THOUGHTS ON LISTENING TO RECORDS

Recently, I was reminded of a famous essay by the German Marxist critic Walter Benjamin on "The Work of Art in the Age of Mechanical Reproduction"[1]—a suggestive title in the framework of this conference. As far as specific attention to music is concerned, the essay is disappointing; it may be that Benjamin wasn't much interested in music, and it's probably true that even in 1936, when he was writing, recordings didn't yet impinge very much on the general intellectual consciousness as a

[1]In Benjamin, *Illuminations,* ed. Hannah Arendt (New York: Harcourt, Brace and World, 1968), pp. 217-51.

competitor to or substitute for the live performance of art music. (At that time, after all, serious criticism of recordings was still relatively new—*The Gramophone* had been founded in England in 1923, the predecessor of *The American Record Guide* only the year before Benjamin wrote—and such criticism was still in large part independent of the official musical and critical establishment.)

Benjamin deals primarily with the relations of theater to film and of graphic arts to photography In talking about the first of these, he says little about the special characteristics that theater shares with music: they are both arts that exist fully only in time, and in that form they are publicly presented, in a significant sense, in *reproduction*—albeit in individually handicrafted rather than mechanical reproduction.

For technological reasons, film rather quickly liberated itself from the task of merely reproducing mechanically the kinds of things that go on in theaters. Recording took much longer—really, until the perfection of tape recording made it as malleable as film. Up to that time, the function of recordings had been—and still is, in considerable part—the mechanical reproduction of the kinds of things that go on in concert halls and similar places: of musical performances, in fact. As with the reproduction of a work of figurative art, there is an original—or perhaps I should say that there *could have been* an original, for many recordings don't in fact reproduce single, specific, continuous performances. Still, I should like to pass over this problem for now, and return to it later.

In that original performance, certain properties inhere that correspond to what Benjamin calls the "authenticity" or "aura" of the original work: "that which withers in the age of mechanical reproduction" is his definition. This "aura" involves a number of properties dependent on, in Benjamin's words, "its presence in time and space, its unique existence at the place where it happens to be." Some of these were touched upon by Richard Crawford in his introductory remarks. Quite a number of them are visual in origin, though sometimes directly musical in effect: let me merely mention one that came to my notice some years ago.

I had received the Boulez recording of Debussy's *Images* for review and was mightily struck by the opening *tutti* chords of *Ibéria,* which seemed to me more precise and balanced than I had ever heard them before. I thought it might be interesting to examine them, as it were, under a microscope, so I recorded them on tape along with all the other recordings of the same chords that I could lay my hands on. I very quickly discovered that it was almost impossible aurally to analyze the first chord of each performance, because I didn't know when it was coming, and its unpredictable arrival always produced some kind of brief sensory overload. (I'm sure there's a perfectly obvious psycho-acoustical explanation for this.) Fortunately, I had laid down two full measures of each performance, so I could analyze the second, and identical, chord—it was easy enough to predict when that was arriving.

The point of this is that in the concert hall, unless one is in an exceptionally disadvantaged location, one could probably not be in doubt about when that first chord was coming—or about when the piece, or the movement, had ended. When listening to a recording, we generally lack all those signals which constitute a kind of aural equivalent to the frame of a picture, as Edward Cone has suggested;[2] the "frame" of a recording—unless, perhaps, it is a recording of a live performance, complete with audience noises, baton-rapping, and applause—is almost always a good deal fuzzier than that of a concert. I rather suspect, indeed, that to listeners for whom the physical coherence of an "album" is a more vivid reality than the concept of a "piece of music," a recorded sequence of unrelated short pieces

---

[2]Edward T. Cone, *Musical Form and Musical Performance* (New York: W. W. Norton, 1968), Chapter 1.

may well take on a kind of inevitability that is almost always musically irrelevant. (At the same time that the LP record restored the desirable continuity of pieces that the 78 had sundered, it imposed spurious continuities on shorter ones.)

There's something else that is rather more important, another facet of the "aura" of a live performance that really does wither away under mechanical reproduction. Let me introduce it with a vivid—not to say violent—anecdote. In his 1969 Harvard lectures, Roger Sessions recalled the day when he

> . . . hurled a gramophone record across the room in a fury, intentionally smashing it. I did this not because it was a bad recording or a bad performance or even a bad piece. It was none of these things; it was Debussy's *Fêtes,* beautifully played by, I think, the Philadelphia Orchestra. I loved the piece, and still love it. But what infuriated me was my fully-developed awareness of having heard exactly the same sounds, the same nuances, both of tempo and dynamics, the same accents, down to the minutest detail, so many times that I knew exactly—and I emphasize *exactly,* to the last instant—what was coming next.[3]

It is, I think, a tenable proposition that composers in the central tradition of Western music did not intend their works to sound identical on repeated hearings. They didn't know that they didn't intend this, any more than M. Jourdain, in *Le Bourgeois Gentilhomme,* knew he was speaking prose. The possibility simply never entered their minds. When I say "identical" in this context, of course, I mean much more than the kind of similarity that earlier centuries probably accepted as "identity." For example, I came across recently the following description, by Chorley, of Giuditta Pasta's singing:

> Madame Pasta never changed her readings, her effects, her ornaments. . . . But the impression made on me was that of my being always subdued and surprised, for the first time. Though I knew what was coming—when the passion broke out, or when the phrase was sung, it seemed as if they were something new, electric, immediate.[4]

It would surely be wrong to derive from this any inference that Pasta's performances were like the repetitions of a phonograph record. Chorley just didn't have any idea of how "identical" identity can be.

Now, in the kind of music of which I'm speaking—that "central tradition of Western art music"—a crucial role is played by rhythm, broadly defined as involving meter, pulse, accent, tempo, even dynamics and phrasing, and related to a frequently explicit and almost always implicit underlying pulse. Much of the rhythmic aspect of a piece is defined by the composer only within certain limits; further definition is left to the performer. Some of this latitude in nuancing is consciously employed, by good performers at least, to clarify the work's structure, to make more precise its expressive character; alternatively, of course, the latitude may be exceeded, altering structure and expressivity. Beyond that, though, there's a lot of instinctual, almost random nuancing in response to local circumstances: acoustics, atmospherics, metabolisms, what have you. This becomes very clear if one ever has occasion to compare two performances that are quite clearly the same in all musically significant respects; they are always quite different in numerous trivial ways.

---

[3]Roger Sessions, *Questions about Music* (Cambridge: Harvard University Press, 1970), p. 52.

[4]Quoted in John Ardoin and Gerald Fitzgerald, *Callas* (New York: Holt, Rinehart and Winston, 1974), p. 6.

Upon repeated hearings of a recording, however, we soon become aware that there aren't any such differences, even trivial ones. And we do this rather easily in this music because there is always that time pulse against which rhythmic events are measured; even—and perhaps crucially—the disruptions of the pulse become familiar in every detail, whereas in live performance those disruptions always hold the potential of being different (and in fact nearly always are slightly different). Rather prominent examples might be the *Luftpausen* in Mahler's symphonies; the first time you hear them, they can—and should—be absolutely terrifying wrenches. Later, even though you know they are coming, uncertainty about how the cataclysm will break and how it will be resolved sustains a part of their initial impact. But if there is no uncertainty left, they are robbed of any trace of their original effect.

What I am arguing, in short, is that the experience of music has traditionally, if only tacitly, presumed the experience of novelty with respect to fine detail—or at least the possibility of it, even if perhaps not realized in any significant or interesting way. And, as Edward Cone has pointed out,

> . . . of all artistic effects, novelty is bound to be the least permanent. We are somewhat in the position of Mr. Gall, in Peacock's *Headlong Hall*. Said he, in reference to landscape architecture: "I distinguish the picturesque and the beautiful, and I add to them, in the laying out of grounds, a third and distinct character, which I call *unexpectedness.*" To which Mr. Milestone rejoined: "Pray, sir, by what name do you distinguish this character, when a person walks round the grounds for a second time?"[5]

The musical equivalent of Mr. Gall's "unexpectedness" is, then, one aspect of the "aura" of a musical performance that, to use Benjamin's term, "withers" away under mechanical reproduction. Benjamin's verb is actually a useful one, for the unexpectedness doesn't vanish automatically the minute a recording is made; it is obviously present the first time someone—anyone—hears it. It may survive still longer if, say, the work is an unfamiliar one and the listener's threshold of perception is sufficiently overloaded that he is in effect prevented from memorizing rhythmic detail at once; even more so if the music's rhythmic character, its relationship to the underlying pulse, is exceptionally complex and difficult to grasp.

In this connection, one might even consider the possibility that some of the directions recent composition has taken constitute, in part, strategies for sustaining that "aura," that quality of unexpectedness, in the knowledge that recordings will probably be the primary means of dissemination for new works. On the one hand, great complexity delays—may virtually preclude—predictability of detail; on the other, complete abandonment of a background pulse obviates any role for rhythmic expectation in our experience of a piece (though I am not entirely convinced that this prevents recordings of such pieces from eventually becoming boring too).

Somewhere along here, I imagine that some of you are getting ready to protest, because in fact you do listen to recordings repeatedly and still find pleasure in them. Of course; so do I. But I would suggest that the nature of your subsequent listening becomes, sooner or later, different from that of hearing a live performance (or that of hearing a recording for the first time). What it becomes is a kind of experience—or several kinds of experience—that was never possible before the advent of recordings. There's probably no single all-encompassing explanation, but I can think of several partial ones.

---

[5]Cone, p. 54.

For example, we may become fascinated by some technical or timbral aspect of a performance: the kind of thing Roger Reynolds has described with Horowitz's recording of the Chopin A-flat Polonaise. I have this kind of fixation on the sound of Rosa Ponselle's voice and on Tito Schipa's lambent, loving pronunciation of the Italian language; on the chiaroscuro that Rachmaninoff brings to passagework, on the sheer aplomb of Dennis Brain's playing of French horn or garden hose. In such cases, we are not merely focusing on the performance rather than the work; we are intent upon a specific characteristic of the performance, and usually one that is not essentially tied up with the work's rhythmic structure.

Vocal recordings present another kind of special case. We know there are many people who respond to vocal music and to no other kind, and we often feel—sometimes with reason, I fear—that such people aren't really interested in music, that they are ignoring the part of the experience that we consider most central, most precisely expressive. But what they are attending to is surely also an essential part of vocal music: a sense of human contact, much more direct and gutsy and readily accessible for the amateur, involving as it does the human throat, words (even though often incomprehensible), and speech-like intonations. This sense of human contact is vividly present in the records of, say, Caruso, Lotte Lehmann, or Kathleen Ferrier; we feel we know these people, and welcome making their reacquaintance, even though we might prefer to do it with a performance we never heard before; failing that, we will settle for a repetition.

(I wonder if there isn't some kind of reverse corollary to this, in the figure of Dietrich Fischer-Dieskau. Roughly every month for about a quarter of a century now, he has come knocking at our doors with a new recording, or a re-recording, of something. By now, we know him too well; he sings new songs but he long since ran out of enough new *personae* to match them, and even the recent introduction of a fresh and more assertive generation of accompanying pianists hasn't overcome our distinct sense of *déjà entendu.* Before recordings, no singer ever presented himself before the public in so many songs; all that was required then was to offer an evening's worth of precise and distinct personifications—not hundreds of hours of them! The undertaking has been an impossible one, and its failure should not discredit Fischer-Dieskau vis-à-vis other singers less ambitious or less favored by the record companies; the remarkable thing is that, every now and then, he can still surprise us with something new and genuine.)

To return to the other side: I don't doubt that, for some listeners (and perhaps occasionally for all of us), the unchanging aspect of recordings can be pleasing and reassuring; they can act as aural security blankets, particularly if they have extra-musical associations. I'm sure this plays a role in most people's experience of popular music, and it is also involved in the various waves of nostalgic reissues that have recently swept the record business: life may be getting worse, but the old records, at least, stay the same.

In another dimension, listening to a familiar record in fresh company can revitalize the experience: not quite the same as hearing it for the first time, but providing a kind of fresh perspective through another's ears and responses.

With all this, I still find there are recordings that I can no longer listen to—not because they are bad; rather, because their strongest qualities inhere in precisely those aspects of performance that decay most quickly under mechanical repetition and memorization. For example, the recordings of Wilhelm Furtwängler at their most individual can provide experiences intense and revelatory on first hearing—but what made them great performances (and many of them are in fact live-performance recordings rather than studio jobs) is precisely what makes them wear out as recordings. This phenomenon surely has something to do with the kinds of recordings that have been prevalent in recent years: for fear of making recordings that will become intolerable under repetition, performers and producers have often ended up making recordings that aren't very interesting to begin with.

Perhaps that period is gradually waning. At any rate, with nearly every work in the standard literature represented by multiple recordings, it should hardly be necessary any more to memorize a performance inadvertently in the course of studying a piece. The idea of the "definitive performance" has gradually receded (even if Bernard Haggin is still sitting over there in the corner waving Toscanini records at us). Perhaps we can eventually get around to abolishing the idea of the "definitive recording of someone's performance of a piece"—spliced, cosmeticized, and gussied up so as to be purportedly superior to any single real performance. In the long run, this effort to make recordings "better than life" may be a specious one, though it helps to justify asking the public to part with hard cash for what is in some sense a wasting asset and is in fact often worse than life. If it were possible to hear a different performance every time we listened to a recording of a work, something musically and humanly valuable would be restored to reproduced music.

You may think that I'm asking for the classical equivalent of Mort Sahl's "Perfect Jazz Record," of which James Goodfriend has reminded us: "every time you play it, the solos are different." Well, yes—but something like it is technologically possible, and some people—albeit quite illegally—have already got it. I mean those folks who, from libraries, friends' collections, and their local FM stations, assemble flexible, rotating collections of recordings on tape. When they get bored with something—a piece or a performance—they press the erase button and replace it with something else, perhaps even another performance of the same piece. It is not difficult to imagine a system of archives, cable systems, and cassette recorders that would broaden and generalize this *sub rosa* practice into a legitimate system. Of course, a procedure for compensating composers and performers would have to be worked out—whatever this might be, it could hardly yield them less revenue than they are now getting from the growing illegal practice. (In a utopian frame of mind, I could even imagine the system involving cassettes that would self-erase after a few days, to prevent anyone from getting too familiar with a particular performance!)

Perhaps this isn't a practicable idea—but I'm sure that thinking about alternative models for the dissemination of recorded music is a healthy exercise. At this stage in the history of recordings, it is certainly no longer technological necessity but rather custom, expediency, and commerce that dictate the present system with its concomitant esthetic effects.

CLAIRE BROOK: You have reminded me of a new distinction that recordings have created—that between a music reviewer and a critic. The record reviewer has joined the ranks of the book critics in considering an *object,* which can be purchased and enjoyed (or not). Criticism of records, as opposed to live-music events, thus becomes much more of an educative process, not simply reportage.

DAVID HAMILTON: Yes. And such criticism becomes a more *public* matter.

WILEY HITCHCOCK: I think that in speaking about the infinite repeatability of the recording you left out perhaps the most significant component, which is indeed not repeatable at all, and that is the listener to the record. He or she is never the same person. If that were true, and if extended to other arts, then the *Mona Lisa* might have been thrown away several hundred years ago.

LAURIE SPIEGEL: Also, one might mention that there is a considerable potential available even in home hi-fi sets for altering the experience of a phonograph record, and people take advantage of that. They want options. They adjust the treble and the bass; move the speakers around; play something this time with the treble knocked off, this time with the balance toward the right, this time with the lights out. There is, in fact, a lot of variety possible, and people exploit it. With tapes, there is even greater flexibility: you can erase them, change them, take out notes or put them in. I even have a friend who is currently putting out a record which is designed to track differently each time you play it, so that while the recorded material will never change, what comes out will change every time. Technology is moving in the direction of vastly increasing the number of options for altering pre-recorded material.

JOSHUA RIFKIN: It seems to me that the concern about the loss of unpredictability comes perilously close to the notion—which I think many of us consider to be specious—that analyzing a work somehow destroys it.

HAMILTON: No, I think this is an experiential thing, not an intellectual one.

RIFKIN: But, just as we like to think that a successful work of art retains its unpredictability for us throughout increased acquaintance, analysis, and so forth, so too I think the same phonograph record can. I've had the experience, of course, of listening to a recorded Mahler symphony many times and learning the exact timing of every *Luftpause.* And yet, just as the work of art can put itself back together again, I have found that it remains as unpredictable on a record.

HAMILTON: But there's obviously a question of inevitability. I do find that there is a difference of kind, as well as of degree, when, as on a record, the performance remains exactly the same.

JOHN ROCKWELL: In other words, you are talking about a sort of loss of innocence; you're saying that the phonograph record can rape us of our childlike qualities.

RICHARD CRAWFORD: One thing that strikes me as the complexity of this conference grows is the tremendous range of uses that individuals have had, and will continue to have, for the phonograph —perhaps uses that we cannot even imagine. I'd like to cite just one, from my own experience, which constituted one of the very earliest experiences I ever had with music.

Fairly early in my life, I became aware that my father would go into a room of our house that was glassed in, with opaque glass, and I would hear music coming out of that room. If I stood outside, I could see shadows moving inside the room. Now, my father worked in a foundry—in a supervisory capacity, but nevertheless a person who worked with his hands. He was not a musician in any sense at all. But I eventually put together what he was doing in that room, when I saw him walk into the house one day with a baton. He was going into that room, turning on the record player, and conducting—works like the *Poet and Peasant Overture,* the overture to *William Tell, Light Cavalry,* and things of that type which he had heard in his youth. I imagine it must have been a very important experience for him. I regret very much that I never saw him actually doing it; he never tried to hide it, but he always did it behind opaque glass. Anyway, two years ago, I gave him a Christmas present which he seemed to appreciate very much: a podium.

VI

THE PHONOGRAPH AND OTHER MEDIA

Phonograph records are utilized by many other media than the sound-reproduction system alone. One session of THE PHONOGRAPH AND OUR MUSICAL LIFE was devoted to such utilization. The panelists included a music-book publisher's music editor (Claire Brook), the music director of an FM radio station (Charles Amirkhanian), a museum curator (Cynthia Adams Hoover), and a film-maker who is also a musician (Allan Miller). The session was chaired by Vivian Perlis, who has been a music librarian and who, as an oral historian, has constantly had recourse to recorded technology.

Claire Brook

THE BOOK PUBLISHER AND RECORDINGS

The particular interaction that concerns me most directly is the one between the recording and book-publishing industries. Obviously, there are functions discrete to each, and there are times when an arbitrary interchange of these functions may have unfortunate results. But, for the most part, the technologies have enriched each other, most especially in the publication of books about music. Clearly, the presence of recordings alongside a description or an analysis of, or a commentary on, a musical subject imbues the written word with a force and vitality it might not otherwise have.

Recordings have, since their beginning, complemented and amplified many areas of publishing. The transition from spoken words as uttered by Mr. Edison to the recording of performed words as uttered by Sarah Bernhardt or Ellen Terry took place fairly rapidly. In more recent times, an historic event took place twenty-five years ago when a little-known Welshman named Dylan Thomas recited a poem of his entitled *A Child's Christmas in Wales* into an oversized tape recorder in Steinway Hall, thus marking the beginning of Caedmon Records, Inc. Since 1952, the number of authors and actors who have recorded on the Caedmon label has grown enormously, ranging from T. S. Eliot reading *J. Alfred Prufrock* to Kurt Vonnegut singing selections from *Cat's Cradle.* The list includes W. H. Auden Gertrude Stein, James Joyce, Julie Harris, Robert Frost, Sylvia Plath, Sir John Gielgud, and Richard Burton. The Caedmon company, which commenced operations well after the era of the long-playing record began, was hardly a pioneer in recording the spoken word. In 1912 Pathé Frères produced seventeen twelve-inch "hill-and-dale" (vertical cut) records of Corneille's *Le Cid,* performed by the Comédie-Française. Clifford Taylor read Milton on two ten-inch HMV discs in the 1920s. The Mercury Theater recorded *The Merchant of Venice* for Columbia in the late thirties. What Caedmon did was to utilize the new technology—which made the recorded product infinitely less cumbersome and, at the same time, less fragile—to achieve the position it still holds today as the world's largest producer of book-derived recordings: more than 1,000 albums and cassettes of plays, other dramatic presentations, prose, poetry, and children's classics. Today, Caedmon's "top ten" recordings include five science-fiction titles, four children's stories, and the perennial and irresistible reading of *A Child's Christmas* by Dylan Thomas.

Other companies have come into existence for the purpose of translating the written word into sound. Alternate World Recordings produces and distributes science fiction and fantasy; the Lion Library of Poetry concentrates on great masterpieces read in mellifluous tones by a former radio announcer (a booklet of the narrated poetry is included with each package); Pathways of Sound publishes stories, poetry, and song albums geared for children; and Word, a Christian communications company, produces and distributes gospel records in a variety of persuasions including contemporary, black, Southern, middle-of-the-road, and traditional sermons.

In all these examples, the recordings exist either as an extension or an enhancement of the written word: the poetry was written before it was recited; the sci-fi and children's tales were written out before they were read aloud; the sermons were delivered (after being written down, edited, and polished, I would guess) before they were recorded for use another day. There are, I believe, relatively few instances where recordings occupy the prime position, with a text tagging along at a discreet distance. However, to begin with one obvious category in which this is the case, there are language-learning records, such as Dover's *Listen and Learn,* French and European Publications' *Assimil Language Courses,* Outlet Books' *Living Language Courses,* and Playette's *Wilmac Circling the Globe with Speech.* Each set of records is accompanied by its own textbook specially prepared to reinforce the concepts and skills introduced on the recordings. They all make strong use of the conversational as opposed to the grammatical approach to language study, operating on some variant of the imitation principle. Related to these are other self-study programs, like those put out by Amacom: cassettes offered in combination with specially prepared texts bearing such intriguing titles as *Memory Made Easy, Managing by Objectives,* and *Success without Stress.*

A second kind of record project which inevitably gives rise to a substantial printed text is the mail-order anthology. Sometimes a book already published will be offered as a premium with the record package. Time-Life Records, for instance, presented Robert Gutman's controversial study of Wagner, John Culshaw's book on *The Ring,* and Bernard Shaw on Wagner, along with the first album of *The Complete Recorded Works of Richard Wagner,* in their *Great Men of Music* series. In cases like this, rights to the book may be bought from the publisher or a special print-run made for the distributing company. A more usual variation on this idea is the "nearly-a-book": the trumped-up, bedizened liner notes, expensively and sometimes even admirably illustrated, inserted in a record package but not available separately. Franklin Mint, American Heritage, Book of the Month Club, as well as Time-Life, have demonstrated considerable enterprise in this kind of record-package business. Time-Life's *The Story of Great Music* is an eleven-album series with four records to each album; each album is devoted to the music of one period, and each contains a specially commissioned 64-page booklet. The albums bear such modest titles as "The Renaissance," "The Classic Period," "Music Today," and "The Opulent Era." (I don't know exactly where "The Opulent Era" fits, because I'm not sure when it was.) In another Time-Life series called *The Swing Era,* which consisted of fifteen volumes, a 64-page hard-cover booklet accompanied each of the volumes. Once again, each booklet was commissioned and contains a description of the years covered in the album and biographies of the artists, with plentiful illustrations. If there is the slightest implication in what I have said that such booklets are necessarily on a low level, I must hasten to cite another album of records, *The Smithsonian Collection of Classic Jazz,* for which Martin Williams wrote a superb, 48-page booklet which offers the listener-as-reader a concise history of jazz, an essay suggesting various listening approaches, historical background, and factual information about each of the selections he included in the anthology. (Parenthetically, I have noticed that Mr. Williams's booklet is available separately. I imagine the requests for it were so numerous that the Smithsonian Institution decided to print an overrun.)

Even as I describe these record-package booklets occasionally dressed up in hard or cloth covers, I must admit that they are not books in the true sense of the word, that is, meant to be read independent of the records they accompany. They are the explanation of the sound heard: the rationale, the historical context, and sometimes even the analytic observation. They rarely boast an author's name on the title page (although Martin Williams's booklet is an exception), for they are conceived primarily as a product-enhancing attraction rather than a thoughtful statement by a specific individual.

Since I am more professionally concerned with books than I am with records, I am more interested in the interaction between the two when the book is the prime mover. The book/record combination which accounts for the greatest number of collaborations today, earns the greatest income, and serves the largest consumer group, is the music textbook.

Let me start with what I know best. At W. W. Norton, a publishing house with a rather substantial music list, we currently have four books in print that boast accompanying record packages. The most lucrative and oft-imitated is Joseph Machlis's *The Enjoyment of Music,* a college music appreciation text with accompanying record albums. Most of these albums have been created out of archival materials and out-of-print performances and are leased to the publisher at very advantageous royalty rates or outright fees. *The Enjoyment of Music* went through two editions without benefit of records. Shortly before the third edition in 1969, a record package was created to coordinate with the music discussed in the book. The idea caught on immediately, because it lent itself so admirably to the needs of appreciation classes in colleges throughout the country with record collections that were uneven, idiosyncratic, and often inadequate. It also made a well-balanced collection of music available to students at a relatively low cost. Now, barely nine years later, hardly an appreciation text is published without its own set of records. Joseph Kerman's *Listen,* Richard L. Wink and Lois G. Williams's *Invitation of Listening,* Roger Kamien's *Music* and Daniel Politoske's book of the same title, Donald Ivey's *Sound Pleasures,* Howard Brofsky and Jeanne Bamberger's *Art of Listening,* Charles Hoffer's *Concise Introduction to Music Listening,* Robert Hickok's *Music Appreciation,* and Edith Borroff's *Music in Perspective* are some of the more familiar recent titles.

The first record/book collaboration undertaken by Norton was in a more strictly musicological area. Parrish and Ohl's *Masterpieces of Music before 1750,* originally published in 1951, generated a set of recordings which have become classics. They are still being produced—with a not entirely happy accommodation for stereophonic sound—and supply, for many, the standard examples in score and performance of the evolution of style from the Middle Ages to the mid-eighteenth century.

In addition to the music appreciation and music history fields, Norton has utilized recordings in conjunction with a new music-rudiments text entitled *The Music Kit.* Within this rather offbeat package—offbeat for Norton, at least—there are three booklets and four records. The records were made specifically to illustrate points in the text and to supply the student with examples and exercises. This particular use of recordings is commonplace at the elementary and high school level, where audio-visual aids abound. I do not know of any other college-level theoretical text in which records are so utilized, but I am sure there will eventually be many. Each year, more and more instructional books are being produced with accompanying sound illustrations in disc or cassette form.

The final example of the book-record marriage chez Norton is a textbook keyed to an existing record album. Usually the reverse is the case, as I have been at pains to describe. But when Frank

Tirro set about to write his book *Jazz,* a systematic and scholarly history of jazz for the college market, he used *The Smithsonian Collection* of recordings as his sound resource, referring in his discussions of trends, periods, and players to the individual cuts in this extraordinary set. This is obviously an enormously practical solution to the problem of archival record availability. There are some historic cases where the cart came before the horse . . . and the horse still hasn't arrived. *The History of Music in Sound,* recorded in the early 1950s, was designed as the sound-mate for *The New Oxford History of Music,* which, in 1977, is still unfinished.

I must now make a short detour in order to express what may be an unnecessary reservation. This arises from my vague discomfort at the idea that hearing is, in many instances, taking the place of reading. I would not be a member of my profession in good standing if that notion did not offend and affright me. The active involvement required of the reader manifests itself in separate but interrelated areas: in the perception of visual stimuli and their translation into logical thought; in the necessity for selective attention; and in the development of memory or recall, the association of visual forms with words. Fewer cognitive processes are involved in the more passive activity of hearing. In this day of television, of quadraphonic sound, and of the transistor that goes everywhere, we have all learned to tune down sound to a background level where we can hear without listening, absorb without comprehending. I find the increasing number of sound gimmicks that have become common currency in the elementary and high schools potentially dangerous. I find the fact that Caedmon Records has five science-fiction yarns on its top-ten list for 1977 distressing; it suggests that the time-honored tradition of reading aloud has gone beyond being an intimate family custom or an accommodation for the blind and has instead become a flourishing business servicing those who will not read. Perhaps, after all, the problem is personal and generational: I really didn't mind when my twelve-year-old son, looking for kicks, began to read Simone de Beauvoir's *Second Sex* under the covers by flashlight; it showed ingenuity, imagination, and spirit (as well as a kind of literary naiveté). At least he was reading. He was engaged. He was doing more than passively receiving.

There is a thriving firm called S & M Associates—the initials stand for Success and Motivation—which distributes audio condensations of best-sellers. They are presently selling well, across the country, with an ad campaign that asks, "Have you heard a good book lately?" Well, I for one do not thrill to the idea of curling up with a good cassette, and I would like to reserve for myself the right to imagine what Dante's voice sounded like when he described Beatrice.

I will close by describing briefly what I look for in future cooperation between publisher and record company. To a great extent, textbook companies have already realized the potential for co-production. Since they are most usually dealing with a mass-market product and anticipate sales in the hundreds of thousands over a reasonable number of years, textbook manufacturers have been able to overcome some practical problems which remain major obstacles for less monolithic projects. For example, the practical problems of distributing a record and book package as a trade item—meant for the general public—are almost insurmountable. Record dealers will not handle books because they are accustomed to operating with a more profitable discount than the book industry allows. Book dealers have an allergic reaction to records, finding them hard to handle and hardly worth the trouble. True, many bookstores in large cities carry records, but usually in a separate department, handled by a special buyer, and serviced by a different wholesaling procedure. Once in a while, a record will be built into the back cover of a book: for example, in Seagrave and Thomas's *Songs of the Minnesingers,* a ten-inch long-playing record makes sixteen songs, specially recorded, available to the reader. In such instances, the sum of the two parts is far greater than the whole, for in amplifying and enlarging on the written descriptions of sound phenomena by reproducing the sounds themselves, a higher order of comprehension is achieved. Another example that comes to mind is the beautifully produced and long-awaited *Proceedings of the Josquin Festival Conference*, published by Oxford University Press in a handsome double slipcase with three seven-inch 33-1/3 r. p. m. records, specially made, tucked into their own box next to the book.

The other major obstacle, as I see it, to enlarging the scope of record-book interaction, is embodied in the words "specially recorded" which I have just used twice. Putting together an archive record presents surmountable problems; making a new recording for a highly specialized or scholarly book, one of limited market appeal, makes these problems mountainous. Costs of hiring artists, renting studios, editing and mastering tapes, in addition to exorbitant record production charges, squelch many worthy projects before they are even seriously contemplated. But can you not envisage the delights of reading, say, Richard Crawford's *Andrew Law, American Psalmodist* with a companion recording at hand? or Charles Hamm's forthcoming book on the American popular song with all the tunes hard by? How much more meaningful to our Western ears would William Malm's book on *Japanese Music and Musical Instruments* be if it were accompanied by a record or cassette! Ways must be found to minimize distributional difficulties and cost considerations in order to achieve an ideal—the natural cohabitation of music and word in an environment that does not sacrifice one to the other and maintains the highest standards of excellence in both.

CYNTHIA HOOVER: A book and record package is apt to be a great problem to a librarian. They often separate them, and then you've lost the relationship.

CLAIRE BROOK: That very often happens. The answer does not lie in ingenious packaging—those plastic wonder-bags that open up to reveal a myriad of things. Some of the stuff that librarians have been getting, from Silver-Burdette and the various "El-High" educational publishers, they don't even know what to *call*. They get a bag with things in it: a piece of paper, a cassette, you name it. They don't know whether to call it a book, an object, a conglomerate, or what.

WILLIAM MALM: The ideal solution of the future is the digital recording, about the size of a 3 x 5 card. You could put an entire Beethoven symphony on a 3 x 5 card, and when played it would all come out with perfectly good fidelity. It would be thin enough to be slipped very easily within the covers, and it's magnetic; it doesn't have any grooves; it's hardly breakable.

DAVID HAMILTON: A historical footnote, about the idea of having a record package to go with an appreciation text: this became possible, really, only in the sixties, with the pop music explosion, which meant that students had their own record players—not just music students but everybody. So you can consider that this is a way in which one cultural development has protected another.

VIVIAN PERLIS: It occurs to me that "audio-visual aids" has become a dirty term in the same way that "music appreciation" did at one time. But I think that audio-visual aids can be enormously valuable, if used in the right way, and certainly Claire Brook has pointed out any number of high-quality examples. Also, in some other areas, recorded additions to printed materials could be very useful. I think of Nat Hentoff writing *Hear Me Talking to Ya*—trying, in some way, to put in print the sense of people actually talking about jazz. That is extremely difficult.

ALLAN MILLER: As an illustration of the way that audio-visuals are taking over in the minds of the young, I quote you a letter I received after having worked with the Denver Symphony Orchestra in a school concert. It said, "Thank you very much for sending us the orchestra. We especially liked Beethoven, because in our class we listen to all his records and watch all his in-school television programs."

JOSHUA RIFKIN: Can we sign him up?

PERLIS: By the way, such august institutions as the Harvard University Press have been publishing cassettes, in what look like book form, of professors' and others' lectures.

BROOK: Yes, there is a series available called "The Expert Teacher" which will give you, without your having to pay his fee or feed him, an expert in any field in your classroom via a cassette. Of course you can't answer the expert back, and you can't ask him any questions. (You can ask, but he won't answer you.) What this is really doing is turning the clock back to the ancient tradition of the lecturer-professor who has no contact with the students whatsoever. He simply comes in with his black robe flapping, reads his speech, and leaves. But now, instead of the black robe flapping, you have a cassette twirling.

Cynthia Adams Hoover

THE PHONOGRAPH AND MUSEUMS

I was a little puzzled when I first learned that I was on a panel labeled "The Phonograph and Other Media," for I hadn't thought that my curatorial duties—involving research, collections, and exhibitions—would qualify me as a member of "the media." But I needed only to walk through the exhibition halls of my own museum to understand why many people would categorize museums as "media." Today's museums are full of sound and flash.

As I thought about the museum and its relationship to the phonograph, it occurred to me that museums have tended to absorb many of the characteristics and fashions of different eras and that the use of multi-media techniques is just the most recent fashion adopted. In this paper I would like to point out some of the traits that museums have taken on through the years, with some emphasis upon those that relate to the use of sound and music; and I will comment briefly upon the use of sound and recordings in museums since the invention of the phonograph. I will include in my remarks some suggestions about how I think recorded sound should be used both in exhibitions and in the scholarly work of the museum.

I start my list of examples of museums reflecting general cultural trends with the eighteenth century. When the encyclopedic approach to inquiry was popular, so was the encyclopedic approach to collecting, and "cabinets of curiosities" began to appear. When the middle class acquired enough money and power to insist that concerts and operas become more available to more people, so did collections become more accessible; private collections evolved into public institutions.

When, in the nineteenth century, Victorian life stressed activities of usefulness and moral uplift, museums became institutions for self-improvement.[1] When the taxonomic approach became the fashionable approach to natural science, museums followed suit. Knowledge was presented as a highly ordered classification of types as seen through row upon row of butterflies, brachipods, and Zuni pots.

An important change, and one that would eventually lead to sound reproduction in museums, was heralded when some curators started to question the approach of presenting objects through classification. They thought that objects should be put into context. Thus, some natural history museum developed habitat groupings; cultural historians turned to period rooms and open-air museums.[2] For some, a natural outgrowth of this approach was the desire to involve more of the senses: how comple it would be to touch, smell, and *hear* the context as well as to see it!

Worth exploring in some detail is the notion of museums as a place for pleasure, delight, and ent tainment. In both the eighteenth and the nineteenth centuries, many museum visitors were entertaine at museums–and sometimes by music. For instance, Susan Burney, daughter of Charles Burney, wrot to her sister Fanny about a visit to a London museum in 1778:

> Saturday morning we spent extremely well at Sir Ashton Lever's Museum. I wish I was a good Natural Historian, that I might give you some idea of our *entertainment* in seeing bir beasts, shells, fossils, etc., but I can scarce remember a dozen names of the thousand I hea that were new to me. [Italics mine]

She found music among the delights. In addition to the hummingbirds, peacocks, hippopotamus, and other wonders, there was a roomful of monkeys, one of which presented the company "with an Italia song."[3] In America, Charles Wilson Peale advertised in the *Pennsylvania Packet* (18 July 1786) that "Mr. Peale, ever desirous to *please* and *entertain* the public, will make a part of his house a repository for Natural Curiosities."[4] [Italics mine] An early advertisement for the Charleston Museum (founde in 1773) also mentions music: among the attractions were extensive collections of "Beasts, Birds, Rep tiles, Fishes, Warlike Arms, Dresses and other CURIOSITIES . . . the whole elegantly arranged in gla cases, open every day from 9 o'clock and brilliantly illuminated every evening, with occasionally a *Ba of Music.*"[5]

---

[1]One nineteenth-century author wrote that "a museum and a free library are as necessary for the mental and moral health of the citizens as good sanitary arrangements, water supply and street lighting are for their physical health and comfort." T. Greenwood, *Museums and Art Galleries* (Londo 1888), quoted in Dillon Ripley, *The Sacred Grove* (New York: Simon and Schuster, 1969), p. 39.

[2]Edward P. Alexander, "Artistic and Historical Period Rooms," *Curator,* VII/4 (1964), 263-81. In art museums, however, the work of art usually remained out of context and was presented as an object for worship in a shrine-like atmosphere. The effect of such an approach was discussed as late as 1954 when André Malraux wrote in *The Voices of Silence* that an art museum divested "works of art of their functions. It ruled out associations of sanctity, qualities of adornment and possession, of likeness or imagination." Quoted in Kenneth Hudson, *A Social History of Museums* (Atlantic Highlands, New Jersey: Humanities Press, 1975), p. 12.

[3]Cited by Ripley, p. 33.

[4]Cited by Hudson, p. 34.

[5]Advertisement reproduced in Caroline M. Borowsky, "The Charleston Museum," *Museum News* 41/6 (February 1963), 12.

Some museums, especially in America, allowed the entertainment function to overshadow their scientific origins. As one nineteenth-century English visitor to America observed:

> A "Museum" in the American sense of the word means a place of amusement, wherein there shall be a theatre, some wax figures, a giant and a dwarf or two, a jumble of pictures, and a few live snakes. In order that there be some excuse for the use of the word, there is in most instances a collection of stuffed birds, a few preserved animals and a stock of oddly assorted and very dubitable curiosities; but the mainstay of the "Museum" is the live art; that is the theatrical performance, the precocious mannikins or the intellectual dogs and monkeys.[6]

A superb example of this type of museum was the Western Museum in Cincinnati. Founded upon scientific principles in 1820 by physician Daniel Drake, the Western Museum soon became a "living theater." Its attractions were waxworks made by Hiram Powers (who later became a leading American sculptor) and plays written by Mrs. Francis Trollope (whose children acted in them). The Museum's *pièce de résistance* in the early 1830s was the exhibit or entertainment called "The Infernal Regions," more commonly known as "The Regions." The presentation attempted to show an environment simulating Hell, complete with grotesque wax figures and mechanical devices designed by Powers, background transparencies designed by Mrs. Trollope's companion, the French artist Jean Jacques Hervieu, and "unearthly" sound effects of a "continuous clamor of shrieks and groans, the clanking of chains, the crash of thunder, the hissing of serpents, and assorted other sounds to terrorize the weak at heart." As Louis Leonard Tucker wrote in the 1960s in a marvelous article about this Ohio attraction, the Western Museum, first operating as a center of science administered by scientifically oriented men, later "maintained a scientific façade, but actually functioned on the premise that a museum should entertain, enthrall, and frighten patrons, not enlighten or educate them. It became, in short, a typical American museum."[7]

Though "The Regions" may represent an extreme example of museum entertainment, a more relaxed atmosphere in museums was desired by those who had attended the International Expositions and agricultural fairs of the nineteenth century. At those events, visitors found that they could expose themselves to Fine Arts, Progress, and Learning in an atmosphere that was friendly, boisterous, congenial, and noisy.[8] Why couldn't their local museums become less sterile and less forbidding?

Thus, at the time when the phonograph and its relatives in communication—movies and later radio—were beginning to reach the public, museums were faced with a myriad of demands: to expand knowledge, to educate, to uplift, to entertain; to present objects as science, objects as history, objects as art, and objects in context. Museum administrators must have been aware of the invention of the phonograph, for it was discussed in leading scientific magazines and the popular press. Some museums even received models of the latest developments in the phonograph from their inventors (who

---

[6] Edward Hingston, *The Genial Showman; Being Reminiscences of the Life of Artemus Ward* (London, 1870), 1, 11-12; cited in Louis Leonard Tucker, " 'Ohio Show-Shop': The Western Museum of Cincinnati 1820-1867," *A Cabinet of Curiosities* (Charlottesville, Virginia: University Press of Virginia, 1967), p. 74.

[7] Tucker, p. 73. For fuller details about "The Regions," see pages 90-95.

[8] Some of these trends are discussed by Hudson, p. 45.

hoped to protect their research that way). The Smithsonian Institution, for instance, received on deposit from Alexander Bell's Volta Laboratory in 1881 a sealed wooden box containing the laboratory's first experiments with wax cylinders.[9] By the 1890s, phonographs were enjoyed by the public at amusement parlors, at home, and at fairs.[10]

Yet, from what I can gather from the few printed sources that I have found on the subject and from interviews with long-time museum experts, museums did not seem to use audio devices in exhibitions until well into the twentieth century. Museum veterans can remember audio exhibits at several World Fairs, but the earliest recollections of recorded sounds in museum exhibits date only from the 1930s. At the Museum of the City of New York, for example, a collection of dioramas of New York street scenes painted by Dwight Franklin had "faintly-played street sounds" that could be heard when the viewer came close.[11] After World War II, museums began to adopt audio-visual techniques. Although I have not documented it, I see the adoption as related to the development and improvement of tape recordings and playback machines.

Today the use of audio-visual techniques is so widespread that visitors can hardly get past a museum entry before they are faced with slides blinking, cheery music playing, or roosters crowing. They can spend the visit with one ear tuned in to an audio tour guide and can buy slides, films, recordings, and tapes as they leave. If they want even more material, they can turn to a book called *Museum Medi*[a] which lists "Publications" and "Audio-visuals" from many U.S.A. and Canadian museums.[12] If it gets launched, a "Fine Arts Center" of a "School of Communications" will teach museum personnel the effective use of modern communications techniques.[13]

Many in the museum world have welcomed this new exhibit dimension. Some feel that it is the only way to reach today's visitor who is "tuned into films, television, and music."[14] Others say that the multi-media approach overwhelms the objects and that museums are becoming a "three-ring circus put on in the hope of attracting immense crowds."[15] Wrote one critic: "the museum's indispensable

---

[9]See Oliver Read and Walter L. Welch, *From Tin Foil to Stereo* (Indianapolis: Howard Sams & Co., Inc. 1959, 1976), pp. 28-31.

[10]See Cynthia A. Hoover, *Music Machines—American Style* (Washington, D.C.: Smithsonian Institution, 1971), pp. 31-51.

[11]Interview with Frank A. Taylor (former Director of the United States National Museum), 4 December 1977. Similar instances mentioned by others were exhibits at the Field Museum in Chicago and the Museum of Science & Technology in New York City.

[12]*Museum Media; A Biennial Directory and Index of Publications and Audio-visuals Available from United States and Canadian Institutions,* Paul Wasserman, Managing Editor, Esther Herman, Associate Editor (Detroit: Gale Research Company, 1973).

[13]The Fine Arts Center of the Annenberg School of Communications, initially planned to be located at the Metropolitan Museum of Art, is now (1977) being considered by the University of Pennsylvania.

[14]James Howard and Sylvia Langford Marchant in "Electragraphics," *Museum News,* 52/5 (January/February 1974), 41. This entire issue of *Museum News* was devoted to "A.V."

[15]Frank Getlein, *Washington Star;* cited by Joseph Shannon, "The Icing is Good, But the Cake is Rotten," *Museum News,* 52/5 (January/February 1974), 29.

role is to provide a zone of *silence* in the midst of the insistent yammer of audio-visual *trivia* which, 60 messages a minute, beats on the American sensibilities. . . .[16] Some museums, without intending to, have created a twentieth-century version of Dante's and Mrs. Trollope's "Infernal Regions."

Some of us find ourselves in the middle. We feel that with taste, intelligence, and sensitivity the new devices can add dimension, meaning, and enjoyment. If sounds are carefully selected and installed in an area where the sound can be isolated; if the volume is carefully monitored so that the visitor is not assaulted by the sound; and if the equipment, tape, film, and slides are maintained in top working order, then possibly the aids could be considered. But unfortunately not often do all these conditions obtain; more often, audio-visual aids are placed indiscriminately in museums. Just as the eye must have had difficulty in distinguishing and appreciating one painting from another in many crowded nineteenth-century art collections where the art was crammed from floor to ceiling, so too is the *ear* in today's museum often presented with similar confusion.

In 1971 I used carefully selected taped examples to illustrate eras, sounds, and musical styles in the exhibition *Music Machines—American Style,* which attempted to show the impact of science and invention on the performance, reproduction, and dissemination of music in America. The taped examples were as important to the exhibit as were the barrel organ, tinfoil cylinder machine, player piano, acoustic recording horn, radio microphone, bubbling jukebox, tape machine, theremin, electric guitar, and synthesizer. The sound itself became an artifact. It was not something that you could touch or see, but it was a project of human art and workmanship that lent depth and meaning to the exhibit. We added the sense of *hearing* to the historical context.

To those of us in museums, the invention of the phonograph has provided not only the possibility of adding a new dimension to our exhibits but also a new category of artifact to preserve and even to create by ourselves. We can debate what the artifact called a recording preserves and must question what is captured on the discs or tapes that claims to represent the temporal art of music. All museum objects must be approached with equal analysis, caution, and skepticism. Things are seldom what they seem. But, with an informed approach, a recording can document the state of the art of a performer and of changes in instrumental sound; it can preserve performance traditions ranging from Appalachian fiddlers through Chippewa singers and New Orleans trumpeters to American harpsichordists. It becomes a primary source, something that can elevate, educate, and even entertain.

In 1878 Edison listed in the *North American Review* uses for his new invention, among them the preservation of languages and the reproduction of music.[17] Even though museums did not incorporate sound recordings into their nineteenth-century exhibitions, they did recognize, early on, the value of the machine in preserving the language and music of the American Indian. Field trips sponsored by the Peabody Museum at Harvard sent Jesse Walter Fewkes in 1890 to Maine and to the Southwest to record American Indians. The same museum sent Benjamin Ives Gilman to the World's Columbian Exposition in Chicago in 1893 to record ethnic music at the Fair. The Smithsonian Institution and the American Museum of Natural History began to send researchers and equipment into the field after the turn of the century to record American Indian music and language for preservation and study.[18] Museum researchers still go out today to record. When they return, they analyze, codify, and present their findings, sometimes in the form of a book, sometimes in a recording.

---

[16]Robert Hughes, *New York Times Magazine* (9 September 1973); cited *ibid.*, p. 31.

[17]"The Phonograph and Its Future," *North American Review*, Vol. 126 (May/June 1878), 527-36.

[18]Information about early field trips from Joseph Hickerson, Archive of Folksong, Library of Congress.

Museums have come to the *reproduction* of music much later. Until recording techniques became more sophisticated, until there was the possibility of preserving nuance and subtlety, there seemed to be little reason to attempt to record instruments in museum collections. It is hard to imagine that a viola da gamba player could expect to capture the unique timbre of his instrument through an acoustic recording horn, when cellos and double-bass parts were often replaced by tubas in order for the part to carry. (And it would be equally hard to imagine a trio sonata with a tuba playing the *basso continuo* line!) But Arnold Dolmetsch, a pioneer in the performance of early music on early instruments, did try in 1921—before the advent of electric recording—to make some recordings in London using harpsichord, viols, and recorders. Although the records were never released, Dolmetsch thought that the timbre of the instruments was reproduced very faithfully. "They don't sound as loud as Caruso's but they are, I think, quite loud enough. They might interest only a small section of the public, but from the educational point of view, they are worth having."[19]

More recently, in many museum programs, musicians performing on museum instruments have sought to present authentic interpretations of music. The instruments themselves have been carefully restored, to produce sounds as close as possible to those originally made. The subtle differences in sound resulting from different styles and techniques of instrument-building and instrument-playing become apparent when the instruments are well restored and well played.

Several museums, especially since the 1960s, have made recordings using instruments from their collections. Performers, scholars, and music curators think that there are still many recordings worth producing from our collections. But it is not always easy to convince museum administrators and curatorial colleagues that recorded sound has any relationship to museums other than as entertainment, exhibit prop, or background filler. Many of them find it hard, if not impossible, to consider recordings—even if responsibly and imaginatively organized, documented, and presented—as contributions to scholarship and to the understanding of musical and cultural history.

I think that we have a responsibility to make the sounds of our instruments available to others. We also have the responsibility to present these sounds and the music in as authentic a way as we can—whether it be harpsichord music of Duphly or band music of nineteenth-century America. And we should supplement the recorded sound with written material that will put these sounds into historical context.

During the more than one hundred years since 1877, the phonograph and recorded sound have indeed influenced museum life. In exhibitions, they are used to serve goals that have been characteristic of museums for decades: they educate and elevate as well as enthrall and entertain; they also sometimes distract and frighten. In the collections, the record machine and its developments are objects for study by the historian of technology and the historian of culture. Recorded sound has also become an artifact for preservation and study. Perhaps during the second one hundred years of the phonograph, museums will develop a clearer definition of how to use recorded sound more responsibly and creatively. I look forward to my role in helping to shape this definition.

---

[19]Cited by Margaret Campbell in *Dolmetsch: The Man and His Work* (Seattle: University of Washington Press, 1975), pp. 209-10.

CLAIRE BROOK: In European music instrument collections there is a wide variety of ways in which the sounds of the instruments you are looking at are made available to you. One that I can think of is in Copenhagen where, if memory serves, there is an earphone device beside each instrument, and you can hear in the privacy of your own head the instrument being played. Now, short of having access to the kind of collection that the Comtesse de Chambure had in Neuilly, where you could go and play the instruments, and blow them, and scratch at them, and actually have a total relationship with them, it seems to me that this is a very practical solution.

WILLIAM MALM: What is frustrating is to be in an instrument museum where everything is "No touchee!" In the Stearns Collection at the University of Michigan, we at least have a non-destructible drum with a stick that you can hit it with.

CHARLES HAMM: There's a marvelous museum of mechanical instruments in Prague, and you can play them all. It's an incredible sound when you go in there and the whole room is full of people playing the different instruments.

JOSHUA RIFKIN: I must report on a delightful new extension of sound with exhibitions: in the Herzog-August-Bibliothek in Wolfenbüttel, Germany, which is the home of two of the greatest manuscripts of twelfth- and thirteenth-century polyphony, one of them is constantly on exhibition. And as you walk up close to it, a recording of music from the manuscript is played.

CYNTHIA HOOVER: I might add a bit about our "Music Machines" exhibit at the Smithsonian. The concept of Muzak definitely had to be dealt with in this exhibit; the museum administrator that I was dealing with at that time was very keen on the notion of including Muzak. So I went and had a tour of the Muzak facilities; in fact, Jane Jarvis took me around. I was given the daily program sheets. When I left Muzak I was given a program for that day in New York, and when I got to my hotel lobby I could look at my watch and see what was on. I remember thinking at one point, "Oh, it must be five of the hour; there go the violins."

The problem with including Muzak in our exhibit was that Muzak is something that is just *there:* it's always going on, and you don't really hear it. How to feature it in a museum exhibit, and yet not feature it—well . . . The solution I suggested was that we build something that looked like an elevator and let the people go into it; there was to be no exit. I also thought of putting on each wall inside this "elevator" pictures of places where Muzak is used—a barn, with a breeding scene, and such. But the idea was not accepted.

VIVIAN PERLIS: Are there composers who have been commissioned to write for museums?

HOOVER: We did commission Ben Johnston, from the University of Illinois, for something for the Smithsonian's automobile hall. He was taping sounds of traffic. But it just didn't fly, or drive, or whatever—it didn't work. It wasn't enough in context. It was too creative for the museum.

ROGER REYNOLDS: It's not really necessary, perhaps, to feel that museums planning exhibitions with auditory components should commission works themselves. But surely it's not out of the question to commission the opinions of persons whose livelihood is dedicated to music or composition. As museums and "media" begin to impinge on each other, it's remarkable what an insular way of dealing with these new organizational problems institutions have. There are a lot of people around whose lives are devoted to hearing, and listening to, and disposing of sounds, and they might be consulted—even if they aren't commissioned to do works.

HOOVER: I couldn't agree with you more. But you often get the remark that Jane Jarvis gave us: you—that is, you musicians—aren't typical.

REYNOLDS: You answer that by saying that you'll ask someone who is typical to come in and organ ize the exhibition.

HOOVER: Yes, but the fact is that people whose ears are not sensitive can't understand that you can work creatively with sound in a museum context.

REYNOLDS: We must become more powerful.

Allan Miller

THE USE OF RECORDED SOUND AND ITS MANIPULATION IN FILMS

The choice of topics and the selection of speakers for this conference has assured discussion of almost every phase of the effect of the phonograph and recorded sound on our musical life except one the manipulative use of recorded sound in combination with pictures. As a film maker and television producer of music programs, as well as a musician, I should like to deal with that subject, and then cor sider some highly personal and speculative questions about the implications of recorded sound and especially its manipulation in general.

As has already been mentioned, recorded sound makes it possible to convey *performance* from one time and place to another, and to assure that the re-created version is endowed with the qualities most desirable to those making the record. Composers have discovered that the manipulation and restructuring of recorded sound, and the development of new sound sources, can alter and extend their musical vocabulary. In the fields of ethnomusicology, folk music, and jazz, it is obviously possible to preserve and study music and events from far-away and otherwise inaccessible locations. In advertising, the makers of commercials can endow the most average everyday product with monumental importance, by providing it with an accompaniment of a huge symphony orchestra.

But, proceeding one step further, any one of these single sound sources can be assembled or combined with others and treated in unusual ways. The possibility of clarifying and comparing by juxtaposing events and compressing them in new frameworks can create interesting effects.

For example, here is a compendium of patriotic songs edited together in short segments to create a panoramic view of the whole idea of American patriotism.

Example: Patriotic songs from *Amazing Grace.*

You will note that the Revolutionary War, Civil War, and Spanish-American War songs have an antique flavor to them, but only because of their content. They were recorded long after the events they depi The World War I and II songs were recorded at the time of those events. The atmosphere of the recor ing is therefore also part of the evocative power of the songs, and this power is felt even though the segments are in some cases so brief as to offer no more than hints of the material.

The preceding example was chronologically constructed. But we have become accustomed to ar and all kinds of combinations of unrelated and reordered material. The immediate and the distant pas and everything in between, can be rearranged, distorted, juxtaposed, transported, and preserved, creating a brand new time-world all its own.

Example 2: Improvised mixture of songs and speeches.

These techniques have created the ability to restructure our experience of time itself. The links are no longer dependent on the logic of the basic subject of the material. Whether the arrangement and juxtaposition works or not depends totally on what happens or does not happen the instant before and after the cut is made. Our satisfaction or lack of it is completely acoustic. What works is what works. And it is the recording process that has made this restructuring of time—for that is what it is—possible.

Before I turn to what I think this has meant for our musical life, and to our more general experience, let me show you an example of recorded sound as it is combined with pictures. This is a segment of a film called *Amazing Grace*, produced by me for PBS. First I will play you the sound track without the pictures, then show you how it was made—the processes of sound recording that took place. It is a fairly naive, uncomplicated example of what is technically possible—a fact which makes it all the more astounding, for me, in its implications.

Example 3: Sound Track, "Chicago Blues." *followed by* Film Excerpt, "Chicago Blues."

The "Chicago Blues" segment of *Amazing Grace* was filmed in February 1976, over a period of two days. Our log of the process of construction might have read as follows:

Afternoon of Day One: Three hours of set-up for a recording session—no audience, but lighting as well as sound—in Louise's Bar, on the West Side of Chicago. The group (called The Aces): lead guitarist and singer, bass guitar, saxophone, drums. Interview all four musicians regarding blues, Chicago, etc. Record track and close-ups of performance for two songs, for main version (against which performance that night, with audience, will be cut).

Night of Day One: Film (with sound) performance of two songs, cutaways of audience talking and dancing, plus other activities around bar, etc.

Day Two: Interview (and film) two of the musicians walking in several Chicago neighborhoods, talking about the area and their music. Record separately traffic sounds, wind, kids on bikes. Also isolate musicians' voices, for use in any acoustical environment.

Thereafter:

Transfer all audio tapes to 16-mm. magnetic track and transcribe all spoken material; synchronize and code sound—music as well as words and effects—with pictures. Screen all material; pick most successful takes, decide on overall format. Segment to begin with music from performance, under shots of two musicians walking through varying Chicago neighborhoods (traffic sounds, etc. mixed in, and the two men talking about Chicago blues, as a way of identification). Ingredients and flavor of the music, their personalities, Chicago, all mixed visually and aurally to strengthen each other. Opening section to last approximately 30 seconds.

Try to find the perfect statements, often from separate sentences on different days, for opening. (Cutting of voices very tricky because of inflection differences depending on part of sentence used.) Match with pictures.

Segment continues as musicians enter bar. We see dancing, laughing, drinking, moving about, group performing in background—an uninterrupted continuation of opening music. What was background to the musicians' talking proves to be the real event with them playing—except that the playing itself is built of picture and sound from separate times; only the close-ups of playing and singing are "real."

For final mix, all sound-effects (cash register, clinking glasses, etc.) on one track, music on another, voices on a third; these blended together, added to final version of picture. Final version contains one song cut from four to two verses, then brief applause; another song begun, but overlapped with start of next scene. Final length: 3 minutes.

Such a process as I have described—essentially one of reconstituting the experience of time—is similar to what painters have done with the structure of space. This is most easily seen in the works of the Cubists. It is the notion that one's perception of an object differs according to one's position in relation to that object, or that the "reality" of one's perception of the object is the sum of *all* these perspectives. Cézanne, of course, who died in 1906, had already explored such ideas, which challenged a simple view of space. In some of his still-life paintings, an object on one side of the picture may appear to be in front of a second object, which is itself in front of a third object in the same plane as the first object.

Recorded sound has changed our experience of the "planes" of time. It has altered continuity, proportion, and emphasis. We have learned how to accept experience which is fragmented, discontinuous, compressed, reordered. Event "A" need no longer precede event "B" to define its temporal relationship to it (Einstein).

The techniques of preserving, altering, and transporting recorded sound from one time and location to another have made possible not only the preservation of material, information, points of view, performance; they have over the past years changed our perceptions and expectations of *un*recorded life and nonelectronically treated experience. The view of the world strengthened by our experience with recorded sound—to which many have referred as an alternative to, if not an enemy of, "real" experience—is itself becoming, or has the potential of becoming, a competing reality.

In fact, the ability to accept this non-linear view of experience leads to the expectation of it, and then to the demand for it. We become distracted from what has by now become too slow and undiverting, and we are left with the impression of a dual experience of life. Our mind has learned to function at times in ways which do not correspond to what is found in the processes around it. Or, to put it another way: sometimes we operate in time one way, sometimes another. Or: some of us one way, some another.

This has at least put many among us quite in conflict with day-to-day activities, processes, and even relationships that must remain continuous, linear, gradual, evolutionary, and organic. We find it more and more difficult to concentrate on uninterrupted events and artistic experiences.

Those responsible for presenting these events or artistic experiences find it more and more necessary to present cumbersome packages around the material, to hold our attention. In the case of televised sports, we first add a host; then stopped action, and repeated action; then biographical material about the players; then zippy commercials; and finally a whole other drama of relationships between several hosts, who joke and fight with each other during the game itself. Reality becomes inverted. The background becomes the foreground.

One hundred years of the phonograph have documented this evolution. The ability to record and manipulate sound has not of itself brought us to this point. Relativity theory, the Heissenberg principle of indeterminacy, notions of chance, probability, and so forth, are all part, I somehow feel, of a process of a shifting view of life. Our musical life, as identified in the title of this conference, is organically interwoven with our artistic, social, economic, and ethical life. If not because of the phonograph, at least with the help of the phonograph and the techniques it made possible, we are proceeding along the path to an entirely new experience of ourselves, and of the world we are trying so hard to inhabit.

APPENDIX

PARTICIPANTS AND SPEAKERS

CHARLES AMIRKHANIAN is music director of station KPFA-FM in Berkeley. A composer, poet, lecturer, and teacher, he is identified with the West Coast avant-garde, promotes lecture-concerts of new music, and has initiated experimental radio broadcasts. With Donald Buchla he produced in 1969 the first quadraphonic broadcast (of Morton Subotnick's *Touch*) and in 1970 began the highly successful *Ode to Gravity,* a series of radio interviews with musical personalities. In 1980, his text-sound pieces, *Lexical Music,* were released by 1750 Arch Records.

DAVID BAKER is chairman of the Jazz Department in the Indiana University School of Music. A composer and jazz cellist, he was trained at Indiana University and studied also with Gunther Schuller Bernard Heiden, Juan Orrego-Salas, and George Russell. He reviews records for *Down Beat* and has written many books, including *Jazz Improvisation, Advanced Improvisation,* and *Advanced Ear Training for the Jazz Musician.*

Composer and pianist WILLIAM BOLCOM took degrees at the University of Washington, Mills College, and Stanford University, and a prize in composition at the Paris Conservatoire. Among his teachers were Darius Milhaud and Olivier Messiaen. Now teaching at the University of Michigan, he is also active as a recording and concert artist. He is co-author of *Reminiscing with Sissle and Blake* and annotator of numerous recordings. His compositions reflect a wide variety of influences, including those of folk and popular music.

CLAIRE BROOK has been an executive of W. W. Norton & Co. since 1969 and is presently their music editor. She is co-author of the *Music Guide* series-in-progress of Dodd, Mead & Co. and was co-editor of *A Musical Offering: Essays in Honor of Martin Bernstein.*

Composer JOHN CAGE is universally known as a longtime leader of the musical avant-garde. Well known also for his lectures and writings, he is author of such books as *Silence, A Year from Monday,* and *Empty Words.* His music usually exploits new sound sources (including silence) and often involve audience action and reaction. His *Renga With Apartment House 1776* was a controversial contribution to the U. S. Bicentennial, and both *33-1/3* (1969) and *Cassette* (1977) involve particular uses of sound recordings.

CHRISTOPHER CAMPBELL was in 1977 a junior in Yale College. A photographer and film-maker, he is an active partner with his father in a firm producing multi-media educational and promotional materials. In collaboration with the Yale Art Gallery, he produced "Seats," an ingenious slide/tape/music event utilizing in surprising ways Charles Ives's *Variations on "America."*

Musicologist RICHARD CRAWFORD studied at the University of Michigan and is now professor of music history in its School of Music. He has held a Guggenheim Fellowship for work toward a history of music and musical life in eighteenth-century America and was on the editorial committee of New World Records' *Recorded Anthology of American Music.* He is the author of the prize-winning books *Andrew Law: American Psalmodist* and (with David McKay) *William Billings of Boston.*

Composer CHARLES DODGE is professor of music at Brooklyn College, having taught previously at Columbia and Princeton universities and held research positions at the Bell Laboratories and the Center for Music Experiment at the University of California, San Diego. Recipient of many prizes and honors, he has recently emphasized in his music electronic means and computer-based speech-analysis and speech-synthesis.

Author, photographer, and film-maker WILLIAM FERRIS recently left the American Studies Program at Yale University to become director of The Institute for Study of Southern Culture at the University of Mississippi. His latest book is *Blues from the Delta* (Anchor Press/Doubleday).

CHARLIE GILLETT, after taking the A.B. degree at Cambridge University in his native England, came to New York for an M.A. at Columbia University. Back in London, he taught at Kingsway College and indulged a passion for pop music. His books include *The Sound of the City, Making Tracks: The History of Atlantic Records*, and *Rock Almanac.* At BBC Radio London, he presented *Honky Tonk* from 1972 to 1978 and, since 1974, has been co-director and producer for his own Oval Records in South London.

JAMES GOODFRIEND became music editor of *Stereo Review* after earlier posts as Masterworks literary editor of Columbia Records and Vice President of Connoisseur Society Records. He co-founded *Listen, A Music Monthly* and was record producer and tape editor for Bourrée Productions. Author of numerous articles, reviews, and liner notes, he is currently working on a *Guide to Classical Music.*

Critic DAVID HAMILTON took graduate degrees at Harvard and Princeton universities. He has served as music librarian at Princeton, written for *The New Yorker,* taught at the Aspen Music School, and was music editor of W. W. Norton & Co. Currently he is a freelance author, music critic of *The Nation,* and contributing editor of *High Fidelity.*

CHARLES HAMM is a composer and musicologist and is chairman of the Dartmouth College music department. Formerly he taught at Princeton and Tulane universities, the Cincinnati Conservatory, and the University of Illinois. He is a past president of the American Musicological Society, with an unusual range of research interests, as is evidenced by this list of only a few of his books: *A Chronology of the Works of Guillaume Dufay; Opera; Contemporary Music and Music Cultures;* and *Yesterdays: Popular Song in America.*

DICK HIGGINS is a composer and author long associated with the American avant-garde. He was a co-founder of the Fluxus group in 1961 and organized the Something Else Press in 1964.

H. WILEY HITCHCOCK teaches at Brooklyn College and is founding director of its Institute for Studies in American Music. He is president of The Charles Ives Society and a past president of the Music Library Association. Among his writings are *Music in the United States* and *Ives.* He co-edited *An Ives Celebration* and is editor of three series: the *Prentice-Hall History of Music, Recent Researches in American Music,* and *Earlier American Music.*

A curator in the Division of Musical Instruments of the Smithsonian Institution, CYNTHIA ADAMS HOOVER has written extensively on American music and musical instruments and has edited two check-lists of keyboard instrument collections. She is working on a history of the firm of Steinway & Sons and a study of eighteenth-century American music and musical life. Two recordings in which she collaborated—Nonesuch's *Songs of Stephen Foster* and *American Ballroom Music*—won *Stereo Review* Record-of-the-Year awards.

WILLIAM IVEY is Director of the Country Music Foundation, based in Nashville. He has an A.B. in American History from the University of Michigan and an M.A. in folklore and ethnomusicology from Indiana University. His professional experience includes work in radio and in record criticism. He has served as consultant to state and federal arts agencies, and is a National Trustee of the National Academy of Recording Arts and Sciences (NARAS). Ivey has published numerous articles on country music. He was a Senior Research Fellow of the Institute for Studies in American Music during 1979-198

JANE JARVIS, at the time of the conference, was a vice-president of the Muzak Corporation, of whic she had been an executive since 1973, and was Muzak's director of music programming and recording She is a practicing musician also, as composer, lyricist, keyboard player, and arranger, and more than 200 of her songs have been recorded.

MARGARET JORY is Executive Director of the American Music Center and former head of the Hun College Concert Bureau in New York City.

Harpsichordist and pianist STODDARD LINCOLN took the Ph.D. at Oxford after study at the Juillia School and Columbia University. Besides teaching the history of music at Brooklyn College and conc izing, he has been an editor of music, especially of the Restoration period in England, a staff reviewer for *The American Record Guide*, and a critic for *Stereo Review.*

WILLIAM P. MALM is a well-known musicologist who specializes in the music of East Asia, particula that of Japan. After teaching at the University of California at Los Angeles (where he took his docto and the University of Illinois, he joined the faculty of the University of Michigan School of Music. Among his many writings are the books *Japanese Music and Musical Instruments, Nagauta: The Hear of Kabuki Music,* and *Music Cultures of the Pacific, the Near East, and Asia.*

WILLIAM MCCLELLAN is Music Librarian at the University of Illinois and editor of the Music Libra Association's quarterly, *Notes.*

RITA H. MEAD is Research Associate in the Institute for Studies in American Music at Brooklyn College and has completed a dissertation on Henry Cowell's New Music Society in the Ph.D. program in music of the City University of New York. Among her writings is the I.S.A.M. monograph *Doctoral Dissertations in American Music: A Classified Bibliography.*

Television producer ALLAN MILLER took the M.A. at Harvard and began his musical career as direc tor of educational concerts for the Baltimore Symphony. He has been associate conductor of the Denver Symphony, guest conductor of the Minnesota and Los Angeles Philharmonic orchestras, and was Conductor for Special Projects with the American Symphony Orchestra. Founder of the Music Proje for Television in 1973, he has produced, among other programs, the award-winning *Bolero* and the Bicentennial special *Amazing Grace.* He is Artistic Director of Symphony Space in New York City.

SAM PARKINS, now a freelance record producer, was long associated with Columbia Records.

VIVIAN PERLIS has been active as a teacher, harpist, librarian, and oral historian. At Yale University, where she has been senior research associate in the School of Music and lecturer in American

Studies, she also directs the Oral History, American Music project. She is author of the prize-winning *Charles Ives Remembered: An Oral History*, co-editor of *An Ives Celebration*, and co-producer of two record albums: *Ives: The 100th Birthday* and *Music of Leo Ornstein.*

CHARLES PRICE, a musicologist with a doctorate from Stanford University, is on the faculty of Bucks County Community College, where he teaches (among other things) courses in the history of American music and rock-and-roll.

Composer ROGER REYNOLDS shifted from engineering to music at the University of Michigan in Ann Arbor, where he was also a co-founder of the ONCE group of composers. He later worked in Germany, France, and Italy and has twice spent extended periods in Japan. Since 1969 he has taught at the University of California at San Diego, where he founded the Center for Music Experiment. His book *Mind Models: New Forms of Musical Experience* was published in 1975.

A musicologist, pianist, and conductor, JOSHUA RIFKIN teaches in the Brandeis University music department. He has written and lectured extensively on Renaissance and Baroque music and was formerly music adviser and recording artist for Nonesuch Records, best-known perhaps for his performances as pianist on several discs of ragtime by Scott Joplin.

Critic JOHN ROCKWELL began his career as music and dance critic for the *Oakland Tribune* before moving to the *Los Angeles Times.* In 1972 he joined the *New York Times* and became its first staff rock critic in 1974, while continuing to cover all forms of classical music and jazz. He also does freelance writing for magazines, radio, and television and is writing a book on new American music.

HARRY SALTZMAN teaches and directs the choruses of the Music Department at Brooklyn College. He is the founding director of the Sine Nomine Singers.

Composer ERIC SALZMAN served as music critic for the *New York Times* and the *New York Herald Tribune* before becoming contributing editor of *Stereo Review*, music director of New York's WBAI, and founder of WBAI's Free Music Store. He also founded the music-theater production company Quog, with whom he has produced a series of original music theater pieces including five collaborations with Michael Sahl. Among his writings are the books *Twentieth Century Music* and (with Michael Sahl) *Making Changes.*

LAURIE SPIEGEL is a composer and artist who lives in New York City and teaches at Cooper Union.

MARTIN WILLIAMS is director of the jazz program of the Smithsonian Institution, where he initiated a well-received series of record albums, including the *Smithsonian Collection of Classic Jazz.* Among his many writings on jazz are the books *The Jazz Tradition, Where's the Melody?, Jazz Masters of New Orleans*, and *Jazz Masters in Transition 1957-69.* He has also lectured widely and has been a contributor on jazz to several standard encyclopedias, textbooks, and many periodicals.

The Institute for Studies in American Music at Brooklyn College, established in 1971, is a division of the Department of Music. The Institute contributes to the field of American-music studies by publishing a monograph series, bibliographies, and a periodical newsletter. In addition to serving as an information center, the Institute participates in conferences and symposia dealing with all areas of American music, including art music, popular music, and the music of oral tradition. It encourages and supports research by sponsoring fellowships for distinguished scholars and is currently supervising the series *Recent Researches in American Music,* published by A-R Editions, Inc. I.S.A.M. activities also include concerts held at Brooklyn College for students, faculty, and the public.